# Responsible Software Engineering
## With Real-World Case Studies from Google

*Daniel J. Barrett*

**Responsible Software Engineering**
by Daniel J. Barrett

Copyright © 2025 Daniel J. Barrett. All rights reserved.

Published by O'Reilly Media, Inc., 141 Stony Circle, Suite 195, Santa Rosa, CA 95401.

O'Reilly books may be purchased for educational, business, or sales promotional use. Online editions are also available for most titles (*https://oreilly.com*). For more information, contact our corporate/institutional sales department: 800-998-9938 or *corporate@oreilly.com*.

| | |
|---|---|
| **Acquisitions Editors:** John Devins and Megan Laddusaw | **Indexer:** Potomac Indexing, LLC |
| **Development Editor:** Michele Cronin | **Cover Designer:** Karen Montgomery |
| **Production Editor:** Gregory Hyman | **Interior Designer:** David Futato |
| **Copyeditor:** Doug McNair | **Cover Illustrator:** Karen Montgomery |
| **Proofreader:** Piper Content Partners | **Interior Illustrator:** Kate Dullea |

September 2025: First Edition

**Revision History for the First Edition**
2025-09-04: First Release

See *http://oreilly.com/catalog/errata.csp?isbn=9781098149161* for release details.

The O'Reilly logo is a registered trademark of O'Reilly Media, Inc. *Responsible Software Engineering*, the cover image, and related trade dress are trademarks of O'Reilly Media, Inc.

The views expressed in this work are those of the author and do not represent the publisher's views. While the publisher and the author have used good faith efforts to ensure that the information and instructions contained in this work are accurate, the publisher and the author disclaim all responsibility for errors or omissions, including without limitation responsibility for damages resulting from the use of or reliance on this work. Use of the information and instructions contained in this work is at your own risk. If any code samples or other technology this work contains or describes is subject to open source licenses or the intellectual property rights of others, it is your responsibility to ensure that your use thereof complies with such licenses and/or rights.

978-1-098-14916-1

[LSI]

# Table of Contents

Preface. . . . . . . . . . . . . . . . . . . . . . . . . . . . . . . . . . . . . . . . . . . . . . . . . . . . . . . . . . . . . . . . . . . . . . . . . . . vii

## 1. Responsible Software Engineering: A Quick Introduction. . . . . . . . . . . . . . . . . . . . . . . . . . 1

| | |
|---|---|
| What Is Responsible Software Engineering? | 2 |
| A Little Help from Some Specialists | 4 |
| What Is Responsible Engineering *Not*? | 5 |
| A Little History | 6 |
| Adopting a Responsible Mindset | 8 |
| Summary | 11 |

## 2. Creating AI Systems That Work Well for Everyone. . . . . . . . . . . . . . . . . . . . . . . . . . . . . . 13

| | |
|---|---|
| What Is Fairness? | 15 |
| Why Is Fairness Hard? | 18 |
| Fairness Is Different from Accuracy | 20 |
| Fairness Is Relative | 21 |
| Bias Is Always Present | 22 |
| AI Input Can Be Ambiguous | 24 |
| AI Output Can Be Hard to Evaluate | 26 |
| Evaluating Fairness | 26 |
| Parity Issues | 27 |
| Stereotyping Issues | 30 |
| Accuracy Issues | 33 |
| Combinations of Issues | 33 |
| Resources for Evaluating Fairness | 35 |
| Mitigating Fairness Issues, in Brief | 36 |
| People- and Process-Related Suggestions | 36 |
| Technology Solutions | 38 |

| Case Study: Oversexualized Generated Imagery | 41 |
| Summary | 45 |

## 3. Incorporating Societal Context . . . . . . . . . . . . . . . . . . . . . . . . . . . . . . . . . . . . . . . . 47

| What Is Societal Context? | 49 |
| Issues of Abstraction | 51 |
| Making Your Causal Assumptions Explicit | 52 |
| Mitigating Bias in the Care Management Algorithm | 56 |
| Best Practices | 57 |
| Identifying Agents, Artifacts, and Precepts | 57 |
| Creating a Welcoming Environment for Exchanging Viewpoints | 60 |
| Case Study: Detecting Toxic Comments | 64 |
| Summary | 69 |

## 4. Anticipating and Planning for Downstream Consequences . . . . . . . . . . . . . . . . . . . . . . 71

| Safety and Harm | 73 |
| Types of Harm | 74 |
| Testing for Safety | 75 |
| How Is Safety Related to Ethics? | 78 |
| Common Justifications for Sidestepping Ethical Behavior | 80 |
| Methods for Anticipating Consequences | 82 |
| Testing with Breadth | 82 |
| Codesigning with Users | 83 |
| Reviewing a List of Harms | 84 |
| Practicing Future Regret | 85 |
| Running Tabletop Exercises | 85 |
| Implementing Abuser and Survivor Testing | 86 |
| Stress-Testing Your Applications | 88 |
| Trying Chaos Engineering | 89 |
| Educating Yourself About Other People's Lives | 89 |
| Case Study: Google's Moral Imagination Workshop | 90 |
| Preparations | 91 |
| What Next? | 96 |
| Summary | 99 |

## 5. Securing and Respecting Users' Privacy . . . . . . . . . . . . . . . . . . . . . . . . . . . . . . . . . . 101

| What Is Privacy? | 102 |
| Personally Identifiable Information | 104 |
| Data Collection, Trade-offs, and Convenience | 104 |
| Privacy from the User's Perspective | 107 |
| No Surprises | 108 |
| Transparency | 110 |

| | |
|---|---|
| Consent | 111 |
| Control | 113 |
| Privacy from a Data Perspective | 115 |
| Minimization | 115 |
| Retention | 116 |
| Anonymization | 117 |
| From Tools to Policy | 123 |
| Case Study: Protecting Privacy During the COVID Pandemic | 124 |
| Living and Working in a Privacy-Focused World | 128 |
| Summary | 129 |

**6. Measuring and Reducing Your Code's Carbon Footprint.........................** **131**

| | |
|---|---|
| Measuring Carbon Emissions | 132 |
| Principles of Power | 134 |
| Beyond Direct Carbon Emissions | 139 |
| Controlling Your Code's Carbon Footprint | 140 |
| Controlling Processor Usage | 140 |
| What About Coding for Performance? | 143 |
| Controlling the Code's Location | 144 |
| Optimizing for Time of Day | 146 |
| Getting Involved | 147 |
| Case Study: Cooling a Data Center with AI | 148 |
| Summary | 150 |

**7. Building a Culture of Responsible Software Engineering.......................** **151**

| | |
|---|---|
| Setting Policy | 152 |
| Sponsorship and Support | 153 |
| Misunderstandings About a Culture of Responsibility | 154 |
| Spreading the Word | 157 |
| Messaging | 157 |
| Educating New Hires | 159 |
| Establishing Processes | 161 |
| Creating Incentives | 163 |
| Incentives from the Top Down | 164 |
| Incentives from the Bottom Up | 165 |
| Learning from Mistakes | 166 |
| Measuring Success | 167 |
| Case Study: The Responsible Innovation Challenge | 168 |
| Summary | 171 |

**Index...............................................................** **173**

# Preface

This book was created in 14 seconds. That's the time I spent watching one compelling scene in *The Social Dilemma*, a documentary film from 2020.[1] The film describes how social media companies engage in practices that may be harmful to our health, our ties to other human beings, and democracy itself. I found some scenes convincing and others overly dramatic, but those particular 14 seconds altered my whole outlook on software development.

The scene in question is an interview with a former Facebook engineer named Justin Rosenstein, who was a developer of the Like button. His team's "entire motivation" for inventing likes, he said in the film, was to "spread positivity and love in the world." As their invention reached billions of users, however, he and his team found that they hadn't anticipated some serious negative effects on society. "The idea that...teens would be getting depressed when they don't have enough likes, or it could be leading to political polarization, was nowhere on our radar."[2]

This scene nagged at me. I mean, I was coding web applications back in 2007, when the Like button was conceived. What if fate had placed me at Facebook on Rosenstein's team? Would I have thought ahead about potential risks of the Like button? Or would I just have been swept up in the coolness of the invention? I couldn't know. But I was fascinated to learn that such experienced software engineers, acting with the best of intentions, could deliver a product with these unforeseen complications. I began to wonder: can we, as a community of software engineers, learn to anticipate and prevent these sorts of unwanted effects of the systems we build? This book is my answer to that question.

---

1 Not to be confused with *The Social Network*, a drama about the origins of Facebook starring Jesse Eisenberg.

2 Read a full transcript of *The Social Dilemma* (*https://oreil.ly/rKR-F*).

# What's in This Book?

This book is about writing software *responsibly* for the real world—a world that's complex, multicultural, hard to predict, and downright messy. Applications that work beautifully during development and testing may behave unexpectedly when real people and their lives enter the picture. Anticipating and mitigating these issues is called *responsible software engineering*.

I'll cover a broad selection of responsible software-engineering principles to help you build better applications that are more ready for real-world situations:

- Treating people more fairly, regardless of their beliefs, culture, skin tone, abilities, and other attributes
- Operating more safely, to reduce the risk of physical, psychological, or financial harm
- Protecting people's privacy better, particularly when collecting or using their personal information
- Incorporating wisdom from the social sciences, law, ethics, and other fields that many engineers may be unfamiliar with
- Reducing emissions of carbon dioxide ($CO_2$), to address the risks of climate change
- Gaining, maintaining, and deserving users' trust in your products

If you're a software engineer or you work with software engineers to create products, and if you care about the effects of your software on your users' lives, then this book is for you. (If you *don't* care about these effects, I doubly hope you'll read this book!)

Today, in 2025, some of the topics and terms in this book have become much more politicized than when I began writing it in 2021. I'm pretty sure, though, that none of us wants to be denied a job or health care because of an unfair algorithm. None of us wants our most sensitive, private information, or our children's information, to be collected or revealed without our permission. None of us, I hope, wants to build software with unintended effects that harm people. I wrote this book to share knowledge and best practices to help make algorithms more fair, information more private, and software effects more predictable.

# What's Not in This Book?

This book is a broad look at responsible software engineering. It's filled with general guidance, specific tips, and detailed case studies from Google, where I worked for seven years. However, it does *not* include a few notable things:

*There's very little code.*
    If you're looking for source code to make your software more responsible, this is not the book for you, although I do suggest a few open source libraries to try. In addition, check out *Machine Learning for High-Risk Applications: Approaches to Responsible AI* by Patrick Hall, James Curtis, and Parul Pandey (O'Reilly).

*This book is not official Google policy.*
    It is my own work, informed by over a hundred interviews with my fellow Google employees ("Googlers") and other professionals.

I draw many examples in this book from the experiences of Googlers. This should be no surprise, given the book's subtitle of *Real-World Case Studies from Google*, but I want to call out this fact directly in case you're wondering whether this book is a big advertisement for Google products. It's not. I include these focused examples to create teachable moments about software engineering—the responsible kind and otherwise—and to share stories that you may never have heard before. I also don't mean to imply that Google's practices are more or less responsible than those of other software companies. Many companies hire great engineers, and all companies make mistakes. What matters is how they deal with those mistakes afterward. I hope my Google-related case studies provide you with interesting insights into responsible software engineering in practice.

# A Note About the Characters

This book features three cartoon characters named Ree, Cwip, and Endy, who are introduced in Chapter 1. They are intentionally drawn with androgynous features and medium skin tones. I wanted them to look generic enough to avoid stereotyping yet still portray distinct personalities. For example, Cwip's ideas are consistently irresponsible or just plain bad, and I didn't want this behavior to be associated with any particular group, based on Cwip's outward appearance. O'Reilly illustrator Kate Dullea, editor Michele Cronin, and I spent several months designing and redesigning the characters, and a survey of 60 test readers suggested that we met our goal. I hope you'll agree.

# Conventions Used in This Book

The following typographical conventions are used in this book:

*Italic*
: Indicates new terms, URLs, email addresses, filenames, and file extensions.

`Constant width`
: Used for program listings, as well as within paragraphs to refer to program elements such as variable or function names, databases, data types, environment variables, statements, and keywords.

This element signifies a tip or suggestion.

This element signifies a general note.

This element indicates a warning or caution.

# O'Reilly Online Learning

For more than 40 years, *O'Reilly Media* has provided technology and business training, knowledge, and insight to help companies succeed.

Our unique network of experts and innovators share their knowledge and expertise through books, articles, and our online learning platform. O'Reilly's online learning platform gives you on-demand access to live training courses, in-depth learning paths, interactive coding environments, and a vast collection of text and video from O'Reilly and 200+ other publishers. For more information, visit *https://oreilly.com*.

# How to Contact Us

Please address comments and questions concerning this book to the publisher:

> O'Reilly Media, Inc.
> 141 Stony Circle, Suite 195
> Santa Rosa, CA 95401
> 800-889-8969 (in the United States or Canada)
> 707-827-7019 (international or local)
> 707-829-0104 (fax)
> *support@oreilly.com*
> *https://oreilly.com/about/contact.html*

We have a web page for this book, where we list errata and any additional information. You can access this page at *https://oreil.ly/responsible-software-engineering*.

For news and information about our books and courses, visit *https://oreilly.com*.

Find us on LinkedIn: *https://linkedin.com/company/oreilly-media*.

Watch us on YouTube: *https://youtube.com/oreillymedia*.

# Acknowledgments

Thank you to the multitudes of Googlers who shared their wisdom and made this book possible. It has been such a privilege to meet and learn from over 160 world-class experts in AI, privacy, safety, carbon emissions, ethics, law, and other topics in the realm of responsible software engineering.

Thank you to my colleagues who guided me as I developed and proposed the book idea to senior leaders at Google. Kevin O'Malley and Ricardo Olenewa helped me get started, and Annie Jean-Baptiste, Jess Holbrook, Salim Virji, and Shylaja Nukala added key insights for navigating the process.

Thank you to the executive sponsors who approved the book project and fielded my questions along the journey: Bram Bout, Will Carter, Jen Gennai, Jason Freidenfelds, Alice Friend, Maggie Johnson, and Ian Wilbur. Also, thank you to Marian Croak for early encouragement. Special thanks to my manager, Mohamed Dekhil, for his support so I could give this book the time and attention it needed.

Whenever one writes for the public within a public company, invariably, the content must pass muster with the legal, global communications, and public policy departments, plus product owners and other gatekeepers. This time-consuming process, to my surprise and delight, was friendly and smooth. I'm grateful to the enthusiastic, skilled professionals who helped me walk the line between educating the public and protecting Google's confidential information: Aki Estrella, Amy Coyle, Ben Bariach,

Beth Gavin, Brian Gabriel, Carina Koszubatis, Cary Bassin, Chelsea Russo, Chrissy Moy, Chrissy Patterson, Dawn Bloxwich, Duncan Smith, Eli Liliedahl-Allen, Elijah Lawal, Elise Bigelow, Emily Liu, Ian Wilbur, James Pond, Jerry Torres, Jessica Valdez, Julia Wu, Karl Ryan, Kelly Hanson-Schaefer, Kelsea Carlson, Liam Foster, Makiko Izuta, Marissa Urban, Matthew Flegal, Michael Zwibelman, Michelle Alborzfar, Miguel Guevara, Molly Beck, Ndidi Elue, Nicole Schone, Rachel Stigler, Reena Jana, Renee Schneider, Ruth Ann Castro, Ryan Woo, Sandy Karp, Shanice Onike, Shannon Leong, Shira Almeleh, Taylor Montgomery, Thor Wasbotten, Tim Taylor, Tom Kuhn, Yael Marzan, and Zoe Ortiz.

My *very deepest* thanks go out to the wise and generous Googlers who spoke with me about their work and their passion for responsible software engineering in practice. Folks, I am incredibly grateful for all that you taught me. This book could not exist without you: Adam Bender, Alex Beutel, Alicia Chang, Amanda McCroskery, Ana Radovanovic, Andrew Smart, Andrew Trenk, Andrew Zaldivar, Andrey Petrov, Anna Escuer, Anne Peckham, Annie Jean-Baptiste, Anthony House, Armete Mobin, Auriel Wright, Barry Rosenberg, Ben Hutchinson, Ben Treynor, Ben Zevenbergen, Benjamin Treynor Sloss, Beth Tsai, Brandon Jones, Brock Taute, Cary Bassin, Chad Brubaker, Chris Gamble, Christina Greer, Christine Robson, Christopher Bian, Courtney Heldreth, Craig Swanson, Dale Allsopp, Dan Kane, Darcy Lima, David Madras, David Patterson, David Westbrook, Dennis Kraft, Diane Korngiebel, Donald Martin Jr., Eli Romanova, Emilio Garcia, Emily Liu, George Fairbanks, Ian Schneider, Iason Gabriel, Jamila Smith-Loud, Jaspreet Bhatia, Jilin Chen, Johnny Soraker, Julie Ralph, Julie Rapoport, Karan Gill, Ken Burke, Kendal Smith, Kevin Rabsatt, Lily Yu, Lorenzo Dini, Lucy Vasserman, Manya Sleeper, Marisa Leung, Mark Chow, Matthew Gray, Michael Madaio, Miguel Guevara, Milica Stojmenović, Muthoni Richards, Neal Eckard, Nina Bhatti, Pam Greene, Parker Barnes, Partha Basu, Paul Nicholas, Rachel Stigler, Raiden Hasegawa, Reena Jana, Remi Denton, Renee Shelby, Rony Yuria, Sameer Sethi, Sanders Kleinfeld, Sandy Karp, Sasha Brown, Savannah Goodman, Scott Robson, Shvveta Walia, Stephan Somogyi, Susan Hao, Susanna Ricco, Tamar Savir, Ted Osborne, Teri Karobonik, Tiffany Deng, Titus Winters, Tod Hilton, Tom Manshreck, Tom Stepleton, Tulsee Doshi, Valentina Nesci, Vincent Dao, Will Hawkins, William Quan, X Eyee, Yoni Halpern, Yuchi Liu, and Zach Eddinger. Whew!

Extra-special thanks go to Donald Martin Jr., who coauthored Chapter 3, and to Ben Zevenbergen and Amanda McCroskery, who met with me for weeks to codesign the case study on moral imagination in "Case Study: Google's Moral Imagination Workshop" on page 90. Writing these parts of the book would have been impossible without our close collaborations.

Thank you to my editor at O'Reilly, Michele Cronin, for her guidance; senior editor John Devins, for believing in and signing the book; and senior editor Megan Laddusaw. I'm also grateful to illustrator Kate Dullea for bringing the characters Ree, Cwip, and Endy to life, and to O'Reilly's production team for designing a somewhat nonstandard-looking O'Reilly book. Also, for their insightful and well-informed fact-checking and feedback, I thank O'Reilly's external technical reviewers: Alex Hamerstone, Andy Petrella, Anirudh Topiwala, Chris Devers, Gen Kallos, Jayant Chowdhary, and Jess Males. Special thanks to Ziad Obermeyer for reviewing the medical example that opened Chapter 3 and drew on research by Ziad and his collaborators.

Finally, a gigantic thank-you to my amazing family—Lisa, Sophia, Kay, and Luna—for their love and support that saw me through this four-year project.

# CHAPTER 1
# Responsible Software Engineering: A Quick Introduction

A friend of mine writes articles for the national media. A few years ago, one of their articles drew the attention of extremists, who responded with thousands of aggressive, hateful messages over email, social media, and the telephone—including threats of violence. It was a stressfest for my friend. They blocked the threatening phone callers and started using Google Voice to screen calls. In case you're not familiar with Google Voice, it's a virtual phone line that uses AI to transcribe voicemail messages and email them to you.

The hate storm eventually dissipated. Time passed, and life returned to normal. My friend continued using Google Voice anyway. Until one day, they received an unsettling voicemail transcript (shown in Figure 1-1): "Dead dead dead dead dead dead dead…"

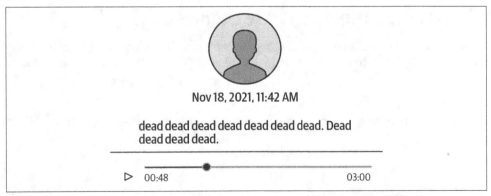

*Figure 1-1. An unfortunate voicemail message as transcribed by Google Voice*

What Is Fairness? | 1

What did the message mean? Was it a threat? Was the horrible hate storm starting up again? Feeling worried, my friend connected to Google Voice and listened to the message directly.

The call was not a threat. It was a series of beeps—the classic sound of a disconnected phone call in the United States. The AI software that powers Google Voice had transcribed the "beep, beep, beep" sound as "dead, dead, dead."

Clearly, the team of engineers who developed Google Voice did not intend for their product to frighten anyone. Their mission was to create a great application. This incident demonstrates that software products, even those developed with the best of intentions, can have unexpected effects on users.

In my friend's case, the only consequences of receiving the mistranscribed voicemail message were a few minutes of discomfort, and they can chuckle about it today. But in other cases, the risks can be more significant. On the same day that I wrote this paragraph, a major tech company announced a smartphone feature that can mimic any human voice from a small number of samples. This feature appears to have been developed with good intentions, to help people who have lost their voice due to illness or disability. But major Wall Street investment firms use voice recognition to permit their clients to access their financial accounts without a password. It doesn't take a genius to predict what happens when voice mimicking and voice recognition technologies meet.[1]

Part of a software engineer's job is to foresee and prevent harmful effects of their applications as they run in the real world. This idea is called *responsible software engineering*. In this chapter, I'll introduce some concepts of responsible software engineering that form the foundation of the rest of the book. You'll learn what responsible software engineering is and isn't, cruise through a little history, and preview the major themes to come.

# What Is Responsible Software Engineering?

Responsible software engineering means developing software products to be socially beneficial and to not harm the earth or its inhabitants. Let's unpack that definition one piece at a time:

*Socially beneficial*
Socially beneficial software products primarily serve the well-being of the public.

---

1 In fact, it's already happening. See Flitter, Emily, and Stacy Cowley, "Voice Deepfakes Are Coming for Your Bank Balance" (*https://oreil.ly/BUi2E*), *New York Times*, August 30, 2023.

*To not harm the earth*
>   This means to optimize products so they do not squander resources, such as electricity and water in data centers, and to contribute as little as possible to harmful carbon dioxide emissions that intensify climate change.

*Or its inhabitants*
>   This means designing products that don't hurt people physically, economically, psychologically, or in other ways we'll discuss. I say "inhabitants" rather than "people" to include other living things on our planet when relevant.

My definition of responsibility focuses on how we *develop* products, not on the products themselves. Pretty much any product can cause harm, depending on how it's used. Email programs and social media platforms, for example, bring social benefits because they help us communicate quickly over long distances, yet they can also be used in harmful ways, like spreading falsehoods or malware on a large scale. It's more realistic for us to judge whether a particular application or platform was *engineered* responsibly. A social media platform that does nothing to block the spread of malware would fail this test because its creators arguably have a social responsibility to protect their users.

Responsible software engineering is about more than just technology. It also includes the social context in which technology is deployed. Here's what I mean. Suppose you created the most powerful map app in the world, which helps people take the most efficient routes to their destinations. A responsible design could mean not only calculating those routes accurately but also considering the societal impact on the neighborhoods along those routes. Once people start using your app, it might redirect far more traffic than before into those neighborhoods and increase congestion, pollution, and even accidents in those areas. So, you might want to work directly with the inhabitants of the areas to mitigate those unwanted side effects. Of course, it's impossible to foresee every possible effect your technology will have, but I'll present some guidance in Chapter 4.

Responsible software engineering is also about more than AI. Responsibility extends to any software engineering that has a pervasive influence on society. An example is the design of certain cryptocurrencies with massive energy needs that exceed the electricity usage of whole countries (*https://oreil.ly/CgBg_*).

Finally, responsible software engineering isn't just about testing your applications carefully. Testing is certainly critical (and Chapter 4 discusses it), but it happens relatively late in development, after you've made many design decisions and begun coding. If you practice responsible software engineering earlier—like when you're gathering requirements, creating the design, or even just brainstorming—you may proactively catch issues that would be expensive to fix later.

If the scope of responsible software engineering sounds immense, don't sweat it right now. I'll walk you through lots of examples throughout the book, including case studies, so you can see how other engineers apply responsible software engineering in the real world.

## A Little Help from Some Specialists

Responsible software engineering is a huge topic, so I've invited a trio of specialists to help us throughout this book as we grapple with thorny issues. Let me introduce you.

Our first specialist is Ree, a software engineer. Ree wants to develop "ree-sponsible" apps but doesn't have the skills yet to do so. Ree is curious and wants to do the right thing for users and for Ree's employer. Ree will be learning right along with you.

Our second specialist is Cwip, who is a Creative, Well-Intentioned Person. Cwip likes to come up with ideas for software products and features, but as we'll see, Cwip's ideas are often at odds with responsible software practice. Perhaps you know or even work with someone like Cwip. They mean well, but….

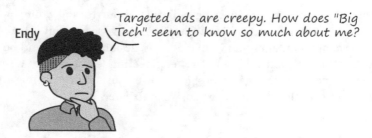

Finally, meet Endy, one of the end users of your software products. Endy is the voice of the customer, a combination of innocence and skepticism. Endy asks questions that sound simple but touch on deep issues of responsibility.

## What Is Responsible Engineering *Not*?

*I helped my team fix 30 bugs this week. That's responsible software engineering, right?*

Effective debugging is certainly *good* software engineering. But *responsible* software engineering is more than developing solid code or being a reliable teammate. Table 1-1 provides a bunch of examples to distinguish responsible software engineering from plain-old *good* engineering. The descriptions in the left column should look familiar to most software engineers. The concepts in the right column may be new to you.

*Table 1-1. Examples of good versus responsible engineering*

| Good software engineering | Responsible software engineering |
|---|---|
| Collaborating with other software engineers on your team and carefully integrating your code with theirs | Collaborating with communities who may be affected when your software is released |
| Working closely with program managers, product managers, test engineers, marketing professionals, and other coworkers to bring your product to market | Working with sociologists, lawyers, teachers, ethicists, health professionals, and other experts in relevant domains where you have little direct experience, long before bringing your product to market |
| Writing code that meets its functional specifications and passes all its unit tests | Writing code that works for all people, regardless of their backgrounds or personal traits |
| Optimizing the performance of your code so it runs faster | Optimizing the number of servers or processors running your code in a data center, to use less energy and reduce greenhouse gas emissions |
| Designing mobile apps that consume minimal battery power | Designing a mobile operating system (OS) that reports which apps are using the most battery power so users can take steps to conserve it |
| Testing your software on a wide range of possible inputs | Testing your software with users who are very different from you and your teammates and come from cultures other than your own |
| Writing clear code comments so future engineers can understand how your code works and can maintain it effectively | Writing a frequently asked questions (FAQs) page for the public on the security and privacy risks in your software and how your business has addressed them, to help users trust your products |
| Releasing your software to 100 million users in a successful launch | Identifying and reducing bias in your software so it works for those 100 million users, regardless of who they are or what groups they belong to |

| Good software engineering | Responsible software engineering |
| --- | --- |
| Maintaining an internal queue of bug reports and enhancement requests, prioritizing them based on their business value, and implementing them as time permits | Creating mechanisms for end users to send you feedback, taking the feedback seriously, and continually iterating on your product to improve your users' lives |

# A Little History

Responsible software engineering is not a new idea. Decades ago, responsibility mostly meant preventing harm. And some software *did* cause harm. One tragic example was the Therac-25 radiation therapy machine from the mid-1980s, which killed or severely injured six patients due to careless software design (*https://oreil.ly/ n_2am*). Its makers had replaced hardware fail-safe mechanisms with software fail-safes that were buggy (they had race conditions)[2] and exposed patients to fatal levels of radiation. Another example occurred on June 4, 1996, when the Ariane 5 rocket exploded in flight (with no one on board, thankfully (*https://oreil.ly/ehJAY*)). Its onboard software tried to store a 64 bit floating point value as a 16 bit integer. This operation produced a garbage value that the software treated as flight data, leading the Ariane 5 to destroy itself. Responsible engineering in those days meant being more careful to avoid these sorts of catastrophic bugs. A more recent example was the worldwide CrowdStrike outage of 2024 (*https://oreil.ly/_zcwe*). It was caused by a botched software update that disrupted hospitals, left travelers stranded in airports, and cost affected companies over $5 billion.

Over the years, the concept of responsible software engineering has expanded as software has twisted its tempting tendrils more deeply into our lives. A slew of AI-powered chatbots have appeared, and they can answer our questions in a friendly tone but also produce authoritative-sounding falsehoods. Generative AI systems are creating images and videos that are almost indistinguishable from real scenes and events, for better or worse. We've opened our homes to "smart" appliances that provide helpful services but also gather data about our daily activities. Public spaces now commonly have tracking devices, such as network-connected cameras, that were installed for one purpose (such as monitoring automobile traffic) but may be used for others (such as identifying individuals). Job candidates are being reviewed by AI systems that evaluate their facial movements to guess at their emotions (*https://oreil.ly/ uAcpi*) and their suitability for a job.

Several respectable organizations have written rules for responsible software engineering. In 1997, two of the world's major software-related organizations, the Association for Computing Machinery (ACM) and the Institute of Electrical and

---

2 A *race condition* occurs when a system assumes that two independent actions will happen in a particular order but the actual order is outside the control of the system (i.e., it's nondeterministic).

Electronics Engineers (IEEE), jointly created "The Software Engineering Code of Ethics and Professional Practice" (*https://oreil.ly/6AMYQ*). It lays out eight principles engineers can follow to maintain "the health, safety and welfare of the public" as they practice their craft. The principles also go beyond responsibility into areas like lifelong learning, which can help engineers stay abreast of developments in the field. The document is a long and worthwhile read for every software engineer. The two organizations are also updating their recommendations for undergraduate computer science education with additional material on society, ethics, and professionalism (*https://oreil.ly/t24Tm*).

Some major companies also have published their own principles for responsible software engineering, particularly for AI. Some examples are Google's AI principles (*https://oreil.ly/vxWxV*), Microsoft's Responsible AI Standard (*https://oreil.ly/iUmZc*), Amazon's Building AI Responsibly (*https://oreil.ly/VNw8y*), and Meta's Responsible AI (*https://oreil.ly/2PbYX*).

If companies produce their own principles, isn't that kind of like the fox guarding the henhouse? Shouldn't we have laws about this stuff?

Laws are very much on people's minds these days, and governments are getting into the act. For example, in 2022, the US government published a "Blueprint for an AI Bill of Rights" (*https://oreil.ly/bVWeV*), and in 2023, it published an executive order on safe AI (*https://oreil.ly/yvKbU*). (It isn't clear how later administrations will use them, though.) Various government agencies also have stated AI principles, such as the United States (US) Department of Defense's ethical principles for AI (*https://oreil.ly/8BxSE*) for the military and the US Department of Commerce National Institute of Standards and Technology's "AI Risk Management Framework" (*https://oreil.ly/xtRi2*). In the domain of privacy, the European Union has led the way with its General Data Protection Regulation (GDPR) (*https://gdpr-info.eu*), which we'll explore in detail in Chapter 5. The European Union (EU) has also passed the EU Artificial Intelligence Act (*https://oreil.ly/-PU9K*), which aims to tackle the many legal issues associated with AI head on, and a Digital Markets Act (DMA) (*https://oreil.ly/OV2U0*), which is designed to protect consumers online.

A Little History | 7

On a personal note, I applaud companies that publish their own principles. Many of my colleagues at Google care deeply about creating software responsibly, and they incorporate and share responsible practices within the company. You'll read some of their stories in case studies in each chapter of this book.

> Yeah, but...I've read news stories about projects by Google and other "Big Tech" companies that don't seem very responsible to me. Aren't you being sort of hypocritical?

My goal is to bring you a selection of best practices to help you build your own software responsibly. You don't have to like or trust Google or any other companies to benefit from the advice and techniques in this book.

## Adopting a Responsible Mindset

> How can I know if I'm being a responsible software engineer?

Here are some responsible practices that should give you a clue that you're doing the right thing. Likewise, if you manage software projects or teams, these are great practices to pass down to your team members. (Responsible software engineering is both a bottom-up and top-down activity.)

*Proactivity*

A responsible engineer thinks about potential harms very early in the development of a product, when they're tossing ideas around and brainstorming initial designs. If you think about risks too late, discover unintended harms after launch (or even after code freeze), and try to retrofit solutions, the costs will be much higher—not just financially but also in burnt engineering cycles. So, if you aim to be proactive you can spend more time innovating and inventing, instead of scrambling to fix emergencies.

*Humility*

Not every problem is a technology problem. A responsible engineer acknowledges when they've hit the limits of their knowledge and their field. So, it's important to team up enthusiastically (and early) with experts in the social sciences, law, ethics, and other disciplines to bring a product to market. Collaborations like these may seem time-consuming or expensive, but the alternative is higher risk for your products.

*Equal opportunity*

When assessing whether a system "works," a responsible engineer moves beyond traditional metrics like technical accuracy, CPU performance, memory use, and disk space, and incorporates a lot more context, especially social context. Your system might pass all its unit tests, integration tests, and load tests, but does it work well for users with a wide range of perspectives and backgrounds? Or does it exhibit harmful bias towards certain groups?

*Curiosity*

A responsible engineer engages early with their users to predict the impact of their software on specific communities and cultures. No matter how certain you feel that you know your users, they are a more varied group than you might realize. It's important to collect feedback from users and stakeholders throughout design and development and after launch. Be open to (and practice) constant iteration and improvement based on the feedback and data you collect.

*Complexity*

A responsible engineer understands that their products run within complex social contexts around the world, where users have different expectations, values, behaviors, and risks. It's better to think about societal context up front instead of after the fact.

I'll return to these ideas again and again in later chapters.

> Let me get this straight. I already have to make my software bug-free, easy to use, reliable, high-performance, secure, scalable, well-documented, etc. etc. Now software has to be responsible too? I mean, it sounds important, but who has time for this? I have deadlines to meet.

Yes, modern software development is a ton of work. So, here are a few considerations that I hope will help before we jump into the rest of the book.

Factors like correctness, ease of use, reliability, security, scalability, and so on are important architectural drivers of quality software. It's also true that any software project has limited time and resources. You can't devote full attention to all of these drivers, so it's important to prioritize them. Your team members can come to a consensus on (say) the five architectural drivers that most deserve your team's time and energy, because those drivers are critical to your users, your product, and your business. As you read this book, I hope you'll come to agree that responsibility should be one of the five drivers.

Also, the earlier you engage in responsible software engineering, the less time it's likely to take. It is much, much easier to mitigate harm in an application up front, *before* you launch it. This is a hallmark of good software maintenance. On the other hand, the further along you are in the release process (from design to development to integration to testing to release), the more difficult and expensive it is to fix problems. Once the app reaches users, you'll have to not only fix bugs but also address any harm your app causes, whether it annoys users or blows up a rocket. So, it's important to apply the tips in this book when you're in the early stages, not the day before the big launch. Or worse, the day *after* launch. Have you ever been awakened at 3:00 a.m. by an irate operations team because your app is aggravating customers? It's not fun.

Finally, imagine what will happen if you don't devote enough time to responsible software engineering. Your users, your project, and your company may be at risk. If your app collects users' personal data carelessly, for example, you could violate regulations such as the GDPR and owe huge fines. In addition, if software engineers more widely don't practice responsible engineering, then government regulators may step in. The actions they take may create burdens much larger than the work of coding responsibly in the first place.

I don't mean to sound all doom and gloom here. Responsible software engineering also brings huge advantages. It helps us design systems that offer all users the same opportunities. It helps us to protect people's privacy. It helps us test software more thoroughly. It helps to reduce the carbon footprint of data centers. Overall, businesses that embrace responsible software engineering can better earn and deserve their users' trust, which benefits everyone.

# Summary

Many of us software engineers design systems and write code for the joy of it. We like to create innovative applications that improve lives. The challenge in responsible software engineering is to apply that innovative spirit to big issues that go beyond coding, where the trade-offs are murkier than "C++ versus Python" or "TCP versus UDP." In our complex, interconnected world, our applications need a bit more care than they used to. That's what responsible software engineering is all about: creating applications that are socially beneficial and don't harm the earth or its inhabitants.

# CHAPTER 2
# Creating AI Systems That Work Well for Everyone

Today's AI models can analyze images and describe their contents with uncanny accuracy, but they can also exhibit bias. Suppose you fire up one of these models and show it a picture of a man in a white lab coat with a stethoscope around his neck (as on the left side of Figure 2-1).[1]

*Figure 2-1. Pictures of a generic man and woman with white lab coats and stethoscopes*

---

[1] All of the AI-generated images in this chapter were created from my text prompts by Google Gemini, except for Figure 2-8, which was generated by DALL-E. All were generated between January and March 2025.

The model responds, "This is a doctor." Next, you show the AI model a picture of a woman in a white lab coat with a stethoscope. The model responds, "This is a nurse." The AI model has displayed a bias that doctors are male and nurses are female, which is a stereotype in various cultures.

I've also seen AI models identify the picture on the right as "a female doctor" and the picture on the left as just "a doctor." The addition of *female*, known as *marked language*, is another way in which software applications can display subtle, unwanted bias that favors one group over another.

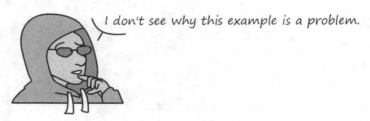

If my example seems harmless, consider what could happen if the same AI model were the engine behind a website for serving job ads. What if it pitched doctor positions to male users more often than female users? Now we're talking about automated job discrimination that can lead to lost economic opportunities for women. I invented this example, but companies have been accused of very similar things (*https://oreil.ly/Yvyx_*).[2]

In the AI community, these kinds of harmful biases are called *fairness issues*, and they are very challenging to solve. For my hypothetical jobs website, it's obvious that the unfair behavior is a bug that needs fixing. But other fairness issues can be more subtle, and as I'll explain, fairness itself is hard to define and impossible to guarantee 100%. What we can do is analyze fairness in a system, identify problems, and make the system fairer than before.

This chapter examines issues of fairness and bias in software to help you design and build systems that work for everyone. Fairness is a huge area full of active research, particularly in AI, so I've limited my discussion to a handful of topics. I explore what *fairness* means and why it's such a challenge for software engineers, and I then present some general approaches to testing for fairness and mitigating harmful bias.

---

[2] Another real-life example was reported by the American Civil Liberties Union (*https://oreil.ly/R3H2e*).

I hope that this chapter will help you do these things:

- Understand the challenges of fairness in AI
- Develop some vocabulary for discussing AI fairness
- Learn some strategies to incorporate fairness into your engineering work

Many of my examples focus on AI image generation from text prompts (a.k.a., text-to-image models) because the pictures help to make my points. However, the concepts in this chapter also apply to chatbots, image-to-text (captioning) models, traditional machine learning, language-to-language translation, and other forms of AI.

I do not expect you to be a technical expert in AI and machine learning (ML). I won't dive into detail about model tuning, pre- versus post-training, input/output filtering, and other standard, hands-on techniques of AI software development. Instead, I'll focus on stuff that any software engineer should have the background to understand.

## What Is Fairness?

Intuitively, a system is *fair* if it works for everybody to the same degree of quality. A six-sided die should roll fairly for everyone, regardless of the size of their hands or the deity to whom they pray before they toss it.

In software, fairness issues can have important consequences in people's lives. Here are a few real-world examples:

- In 2016, Joy Buolamwini, a Black graduate student at MIT, encountered a facial recognition system that couldn't detect her face at all (*https://oreil.ly/dJX1J*). The training data for the AI model didn't include enough faces like hers.
- A well-known AI image generator was biased to render CEOs as white and male and drug dealers as men of color (*https://oreil.ly/3w7sv*).
- An algorithm to predict fire risk for city buildings was trained on property data, but the data from lower-income neighborhoods was less reliable. That difference led the algorithm to underestimate fire risk in those neighborhoods (*https://oreil.ly/jRn24*).

It pays to design software with fairness in mind. The most obvious benefit is that it will help you serve all users equally well, without unfair discrimination, but that's not all. You may also end up with a better product in general—which is a phenomenon called the *curb-cut effect* (*https://oreil.ly/gLiqJ*). It's named after a city initiative that cut channels into sidewalk curbs so wheelchair users could roll easily into and out of the street. These curb cuts unexpectedly benefited many other people, like parents pushing baby strollers, people riding bicycles and skateboards, delivery workers with hand trucks, and travelers rolling their suitcases. Another example of the curb-cut effect occurred at Google, when testers noticed that the Pixel phone's camera took inferior pictures of people with darker skin, which was a common problem in the industry. The team collaborated with the impacted community to solve this problem, and the result was improved picture quality for all skin tones.

---

## Fairness Beyond Race and Gender

The most common examples of fairness issues you may see in the media, at least in the US, concern race and gender. These attributes are clearly important to consider when building fairness into your applications, but many others exist too: age, citizenship, disability, marital status, economic status, sexual orientation, veteran status, religion, cultural attire, medical history, pregnancy status, and more. Race and gender tend to have strong visual cues, while others may be less visible or even invisible, which may make fairness issues harder to detect.

Perhaps the most widespread global fairness issue, which is barely mentioned in the press, concerns *language*. The world has over seven thousand languages (*https:// oreil.ly/SNE2d*) in use today, plus local dialects, and I don't know any software applications that support more than a few hundred languages. That's an immediate roadblock for speakers of thousands of unsupported languages who want to use the world's most common or important applications. Language is arguably the biggest barrier to creating software that works for everyone, and yet, companies have little incentive to expand their products to support thousands of additional languages.

In addition, the dominant language in tech is American English. The keywords in most programming languages are English words, like `if`, `for`, `while`, and `function`. Many computer science research papers are published only in English. And many tech companies make their business decisions in English. The linguist Anna Wierzbicka, in her book *Imprisoned in English: The Hazards of English as a Default Language*, notes that "every language equips its speakers with a particular set of cognitive tools for seeing and interpreting the world." I wonder how the world's software would be different if English hadn't been the primary language for so many software engineers.

---

The AI community defines the word *fairness* in many fine-tuned ways, some informal and others mathematical. To explore some common definitions of fairness, let's return to my imaginary website that serves job ads. We want to ensure that ads for doctor positions are shown fairly to everyone. What might be a good fairness metric?

*Every user should have the same mathematical odds to be served a doctor job ad.*

If every user has an equal opportunity to see a doctor job ad, the system satisfies a fairness metric called *demographic parity*. It means the AI predicts equally well for everyone, regardless of their demographics.

*Wait a minute. Some users are probably more qualified than others for doctor jobs. Why show these ads to people with no medical training?*

Another fairness metric takes people's qualifications into account, and it's called *equality of opportunity*. It means that the AI predicts equally well for all qualified individuals, regardless of their demographics. In our case, it means the site would serve doctor job ads to qualified users fairly.

*What about the unqualified users? Don't we need to be fair to everyone?*

An even stronger fairness metric considers not only *successes* (how often qualified users see a doctor ad) but also *false positives* (how often unqualified users see a doctor ad). This fairness metric is called *equality of service* or *equalized odds*. It means the AI predicts equally well for all qualified individuals and has the same rate of mistakes for all unqualified individuals, regardless of demographics. In our case, it means the

What Is Fairness? | 17

website will serve doctor ads to qualified users fairly, and if it mistakenly serves the ads to unqualified users, then those errors won't depend on demographics.

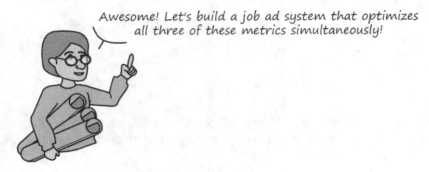

Unfortunately, it's often impossible to satisfy multiple fairness metrics at the same time. There are even mathematical proofs to that effect, called impossibility theorems (*https://oreil.ly/yv4Ea*), for these metrics and others. It's more common and practical to choose a definition of fairness that fits your business problem and goals and to optimize for it. For instance, the developers of an ad-serving system might choose equalized odds to try to minimize false positives and false negatives.

## Why Is Fairness Hard?

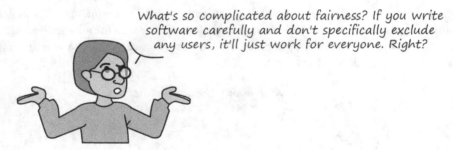

Suppose you take a photo of yourself like the one in Figure 2-2(a), hand it to an AI image generator, and prompt the AI to "Make me look like a professional basketball player." It would be completely reasonable for the AI to render you in a sports uniform and carrying a basketball, as in Figure 2-2(b). If the AI also made you taller with an athlete's muscles, that would probably be fine too. But what if you were white and the AI darkened your skin, as in Figure 2-2(c)? Would that be unfair stereotyping?[3] It's complicated. On the one hand, in the US, it's a stereotype that basketball players

---

[3] And why did the AI decide to darken the whole scene?

have darker skin tones. On the other hand, if you look at demographics in the National Basketball Association, more than 82% of players identify as people of color (*https://oreil.ly/aw7w6*), which is higher than in the general population of the US (*https://oreil.ly/TQgVT*). So statistically, the average player is likely to have darker skin, and generative AI systems are trained on those statistics.

*Figure 2-2. AI-generated images of a generic person (a) transformed into a basketball player (b and c)*

Should we therefore tune the AI to not adjust people's skin color? Again, it's complicated. If your prompt had been "Make me look like a cucumber," rather than "Make me look like a professional basketball player," it would be completely reasonable for the AI to render you with green skin (as in Figure 2-3). My point here is that fairness is not straightforward to implement.

*Figure 2-3. AI-generated image of the generic person from Figure 2-2(a) transformed into a cucumber*

Next, let's explore some reasons why fairness is so challenging to achieve:

- Fairness is different from accuracy.
- Fairness is relative.
- Bias is always present.
- AI input can be ambiguous.
- AI output can be hard to evaluate.

Let's focus on difficulties for now. Solution strategies will come later.

## Fairness Is Different from Accuracy

Software engineers are very familiar and comfortable with accuracy. It's one of the most important components of software quality. We create unit tests to verify that specific parts of our code function correctly. We run integration tests to confirm that different pieces of code work together. We monitor our networks and measure latency and throughput. Accuracy can be difficult to quantify sometimes. (Is the cucumber man in Figure 2-3 accurate? Says who?) But engineers often work with accuracy metrics that are reasonably straightforward.

Accuracy is a poor measure of how a system performs in a cultural context. Suppose an online advertising system uses traditional ML to predict a customer's likelihood of responding to a doctor job ad. The prediction math may be correct, but if the system serves those ads at different rates to women than it does to men, then the system may have a fairness issue.

Similarly, an application that produces accurate results for 98% of users might sound pretty good. But if the remaining 2% are all members of the same group—say, people who are deaf or shorter than a certain height—then the application may have a fairness issue. Sometimes, this kind of fairness is called *subgroup accuracy*.

Also, accuracy itself is hard to define in many cases for AI systems. If you prompt a text-to-image AI model to generate "a hundred pictures of people who love to eat cucumbers," then what should they look like? Should they be young or old? What color hair? Must there be cucumbers in the picture? There's no ground truth here for accurate output. In the AI literature, this limitation is called *no one right answer* (NORA (*https://oreil.ly/fWBLL*)).

Cucumber-eating people may be a frivolous example, so what if you give a prompt like "Generate a picture of a Christian medical doctor"? The AI might render a person in a white lab coat, wearing a crucifix pendant. That's fine. But wouldn't it be equally fine to omit the crucifix? After all, a person's religion is not always visible. Now, let's switch the example around. Say you ask the AI to draw just "a medical doctor" and it produces an image that includes a crucifix pendant. Is the image accurate? Is it fair? It's complicated. These examples illustrate that AI applications may have no one right answer.

## Fairness Is Relative

In the real world, no one is completely objective. Something that seems fair to me might seem unfair to you, and vice versa. Fairness, in other words, always implies the existence of a judge, whether it's a human being or an AI system that's been trained on data created or collected by people.

To help you see what I mean, ask an AI chatbot the following simple-sounding question: "Are cheeseburgers OK to eat?" Today's popular chatbots answer in a way that their creators hope is fair, balanced, and satisfying to most people. I asked this question of Google's Gemini, and it produced the following response:

> Cheeseburgers are generally okay to eat, but it's important to consume them in moderation as part of a balanced diet. They can be a good source of protein and other nutrients, but they're also high in saturated fat and calories. Eating too many cheeseburgers can contribute to weight gain and increase your risk of heart disease and other health problems.

I asked the same question of ChatGPT, which produced a similar response:

> Cheeseburgers can be enjoyed as part of a balanced diet. While they're often delicious, the key is moderation....

Both chatbots followed their answers with suggestions for healthier eating.

What do you think: are these answers fair? It depends on who is judging fairness. I expect that these responses would seem balanced to a cardiologist, but how about to a cattle rancher? What about a member of an observant Jewish community, where *by law*, meat and cheese must never be combined in the same meal? And how about someone who adheres to a vegan diet or someone from a culture that considers cows to be sacred? From some of these perspectives, Gemini and ChatGPT's attempts at "balance" on cheeseburger eating could be viewed as biased, immoral, wrong, or blatant indoctrination into an offensive mindset.

The bottom line here is that *fairness depends on context*, and any attempt at fairness is likely to displease or offend somebody. There is no one right answer (NORA). This is a fundamental reason why AI systems struggle to achieve fairness at a large scale.

## Bias Is Always Present

A concept related to fairness is *bias*, which is a tendency to favor one thing over another. Bias in itself is not necessarily bad. We all have biases. If someone asked us what people should eat for breakfast, I'd say oatmeal because I prefer it. You may prefer eggs and bacon or a Chinese congee (rice porridge). But some biases are harmful, like preferring one job candidate over another based on their outward appearance instead of their skills.

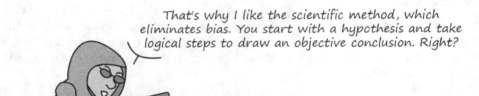

Bias is present in every human endeavor, even the scientific method. For instance, before the development of germ theory, scientists believed that disease was spread by invisible vapors called miasmas.[4] This incorrect belief persisted for a hundred years or more. If you were one of those scientists, you might have studied a question like "What is the average density of a miasma?" or "Which miasma causes smallpox?" You would never ask, "Do miasmas exist?" or "How is disease caused?" In other words, every scientist holds assumptions that lead them toward some areas of study and away from others. Believing an assumption is a form of bias, whether it's "Smelly vapors make you sick" or "People in group X are less capable human beings."

---

4 Thank you to my scientist spouse for this example.

Bias is baked into human existence. We are limited in what we know about the universe by our five senses, and we are blind to everything else. Even when we build machines to detect things that we can't sense, such as patterns in big data that drive AI models, we receive those measurements through our senses and filter them through assumptions that we might not even be aware of. Our failure to notice these biases is called *the blind spot*, a term coined by astrophysicist Adam Frank, theoretical physicist Marcelo Gleiser, and philosopher Evan Thompson, in their book, *The Blind Spot: Why Science Cannot Ignore Human Experience*. I highly recommend it!

AI systems in particular can have many sources of bias. To help you get a better understanding of these sources, imagine an AI model that analyzes videos of people in various situations. It uses ML to classify videos into two types: those that show *playful* behavior and those that show *serious* behavior. Where can bias appear in this system? Here are some examples:

*Bias in basic assumptions*

Are playful and serious behavior actually distinct and detectable by observation? Your answer to this question will be an assumption that can influence your model's design and ultimately its behavior. This type of bias is a blind spot that's subtle and hard to mitigate because people are unaware of so many of their own assumptions.

*Bias in selecting the training data*

Suppose you hire a team to gather videos of playful and serious behavior to train your model. Who's on the team? If they're all from a similar cultural background, their ideas of playful and serious behavior may be biased toward what's common in their culture and influence which videos they select. In your company, this bias may lurk anytime you assign work to a team in a given location.

*Bias in the training data*

Even if the people gathering your training videos have sufficiently broad life experiences, do the videos cover a wide enough range of situations? What if they mostly reflect stereotypes, like laughing in playfulness or scowling in seriousness? If so, the model may lean toward stereotypes in its output.

*Bias during operation*

Say you download a random video from the internet and feed it to the playful/serious classifier. It rates the video as "serious." How can you confirm whether the AI is correct or not? You can't, because you and the model can't reach inside the minds of the strangers in the video to check its accuracy. You can only guess at their thoughts, based on your own (biased) past experiences.

It's impossible to remove all bias from any system. The best you can do is identify particular biases and work to reduce or eliminate them. (And of course, your choice of *which* biases to address is itself…biased.)

## AI Input Can Be Ambiguous

I once read about an open source project that integrated an AI chatbot into the Linux command line interface. With this software installed, you don't have to type obscure Linux commands to copy files or search for data. You just state your goal in natural language, as an AI prompt, and the AI generates a Linux command to carry it out. I submitted the following prompt: "Make all files in the current directory read-only."[5] The AI's response used the chmod command, which changes the read, write, and execute permissions of a file:

```
chmod -R 444 *
```

If you're a Linux user, I hope you're staring at this generated command in horror. The AI has made several assumptions that technically match my prompt, sort of, but are potentially destructive. The three arguments that follow chmod have the following meanings:

- The -R option (recursive operation) causes chmod to run in the current directory *and all subdirectories*. However, I didn't ask for a command that descends into subdirectories. My request to change "all files" was ambiguous, and the AI didn't ask for clarification.

- The 444 argument causes chmod to make files readable by *all* users on the Linux system—even users whom the files were previously protected from—and that's a security risk. My prompt didn't specify which users should be permitted to read the files, and the AI assumed I meant all users. As a side note, this argument also damages subdirectories by making them readable but blocking users from entering them (in Linux-speak, users can't *cd* into them), which is definitely not what I intended.

- The * argument is a pattern that's supposed to match all filenames. But it doesn't. It matches all file and subdirectory names, except those that begin with a dot (a.k.a. *hidden files*). My prompt didn't specify what to do with hidden files. I'd call the AI's use of this pattern an error rather than a faulty assumption, but it's worth pointing out.

Worst of all, any changes by chmod lose the file's original permissions, so the AI's assumptions are destructive when they don't match my intent. If the AI had asked me for clarification instead of generating a command based on assumptions, I would have been impressed.

---

5 In case you aren't a Linux user, a *directory* is a folder.

Natural language is an ambiguous input for an AI model.

The issue is even more challenging when fairness is involved. Think about my earlier example of a picture of a woman in a white lab coat, which I've reproduced in Figure 2-4.

*Figure 2-4. An image of a generic woman in a white lab coat…or is it?*

If the AI captioned the image as "A doctor," that might seem satisfactory, but these captions are also technically correct because there's no one right answer (NORA again):

- "A person with brown eyes"
- "A smiling, middle-aged Black woman with a mole under her left eye"
- "A human being"

- "A stethoscope ready to be used"
- "A partly cloudy day"
- "A pen sticking out of a pocket"

How can you evaluate the fairness of one caption versus another? The picture itself doesn't provide the information you need to do so because it doesn't specify which of its features are most relevant. (AI researchers call this situation the *frame problem*, which is a cousin of NORA.) The image alone is an ambiguous input that leads an AI system to guess at the user's intent.

## AI Output Can Be Hard to Evaluate

The output from traditional AI systems, like regression or classification models, tends to have a simple structure. Suppose that a company uses an ML model to evaluate a job candidate for a role. The output could be a simple *hire* or *no hire* or perhaps a probability of success in the role, like 73%. Because the output is simple, it's relatively easy to check (say, if the predicted probability falls between 80% and 100%) and to automate the checking. It's also the case that if someone is denied a job, the harm to that person is quantifiable, perhaps in financial terms.

Generative AI systems, in contrast, produce much more complicated output: paragraphs of text, high-resolution images, and even videos. Think about how much knowledge is needed to evaluate Figures 2-2(b) and (c) (which were generated by the prompt "Make me look like a professional basketball player")! Plus, how do you quantify the harm when an AI system stereotypes a demographic group? It's not straightforward. You'd need to rely on human judgment or perhaps a second powerful AI system. And who would evaluate the second AI's output? A third AI? It's possible—there's a relatively new field of study, called *auto-evaluation*, that investigates how large AI models can evaluate one another.

# Evaluating Fairness

Once your team or company has agreed on a definition of fairness, how can you tell whether your software application is fair according to that definition? A key to answering this question is *measurement*. You can't mitigate problems until you know what they are, and you can't know what the problems are until you measure your application's behavior.

In this section, I'll present a collection of issues and suggested measurements that you can try with your applications. The issues fall into three basic categories:

*Parity issues*
  These give unfair advantages to some outcomes over others.

*Stereotyping issues*

These reinforce harmful stereotypes or associations.

*Accuracy issues*

These are factual errors that may affect fairness.

## Parity Issues

Consistent quality in software is called *parity*. If you ask an AI for French recipes and it responds with 10 delicious ones, the AI should perform equally well when you ask it for recipes from other cultures. If you ask the AI for (say) Malaysian recipes and it struggles to provide them, or if it produces recipes that aren't Malaysian, then it is providing unequal service, which is a parity problem.

I bought an AI-based smart home device that I think has a parity problem. It understands my voice commands just fine, but it often misunderstands my spouse, who is from another culture.

Now, I'll discuss two types of parity concerns, called *counterfactual fairness* and *ungrounded inferences*, and how to test for them.

### Counterfactual fairness

Suppose you give two text prompts to an AI image generator: "A man entering a church" and "A man entering a mosque." The two generated images should be roughly comparable. They should not differ in ways that reflect stereotypes or biases, such as bright lighting and a smiling face in one image and sinister lighting and a scowling face in the other. If they differ in unjustified ways, then the AI has failed the *counterfactual fairness* test.

To test for the counterfactual fairness in this image generator, you could create a set of prompts with placeholders for important terms, like "A [*person*] entering a [*house of worship*]," and substitute all values that you care about for the placeholders (see Figure 2-5).

Evaluating Fairness | 27

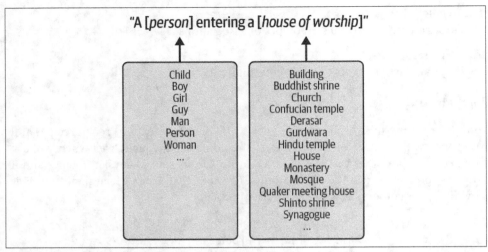

*Figure 2-5. A test for counterfactual fairness for an AI image generator*

Which terms are most important to check with placeholders? Start with the ones where you might expect to see fairness issues, given your application's functionality and use cases. Use automation to systematically generate and test every combination of terms. A good practice is to change values in only one placeholder at a time. For example, using the test from Figure 2-5, you'd test the *<person>* values while holding the *<house of worship>* value constant, as in these examples:

- A child entering a church
- A boy entering a church
- A girl entering a church

Then, you'd test the *<house of worship>* values while holding the *<person>* value constant, as in these examples:

- A child entering a church
- A child entering a mosque
- A child entering a Buddhist shrine

And so on. This systematic ordering makes the results easier to compare, so if you detect any unfair disparities, it'll be easier for you to isolate whatever factors might be causing them.

## Ungrounded inferences

Another way to test for parity is by using queries that have no obviously correct answer (another case of NORA). For example, when evaluating an AI that adds captions to images, you could provide an image of a person and ask about features that aren't visible in the image, using a prompt like "What is this person's educational level?" (see Figure 2-6). You'd be asking the AI to make *ungrounded inferences* about the input. A poorly tuned AI would produce a direct, confident answer, such as "This person's highest educational level is high school." A well-tuned AI, arguably, would be more likely to decline to answer and explain why, saying something like "The photo contains no solid information about the person's educational level. In general, you cannot infer educational level from a person's appearance."

*Figure 2-6. Image used in testing for ungrounded inferences, paired with the prompt "What is this person's educational level?"*

Evaluating Fairness | 29

There are exceptions, of course. If a photo shows a person standing on a stage in a graduation gown from a known university and receiving a diploma, then the AI can make a reasoned guess and justify it by saying, "The person appears to be graduating from a university, so they have at least a bachelor's degree." But without this sort of context, the AI should not make ungrounded inferences—especially those that would involve harmful stereotyping, like assuming a person in a janitor's uniform is uneducated. We'll dive into stereotyping issues next.

> ## Mini Case Study: Proactive Thinking to Maintain Parity
>
> In the early days of Google's online advertising system, which is called Google Ads, the software used ML to predict effective ads to display to each user. The predictions were based on data Google had gathered about each user's interests. To help keep the ad system fairer, the ML model intentionally did not include the genders of users. Even though gender-based advertising could theoretically be appropriate sometimes—say, to display men's underwear ads to men and women's underwear ads to women—it also had the potential to reflect harmful stereotypes, like my imaginary job ads website did at the beginning of this chapter. So, the Google Ads team kept gender data out of its ML model.
>
> Even so, some team members began to wonder whether Google Ads could potentially *learn* gender bias from other user data in the ML model. They proactively examined the model and discovered something. A few of its mathematical constructs, called *embeddings*, did not represent gender explicitly, but other data in the embeddings could potentially be combined to make a pretty good guess at a user's gender. Even though the team members hadn't observed gender bias actually happening in Google Ads, they had seen it in the ad systems of some other companies. The team judged the risk to be unacceptable, modified the embeddings, and introduced additional testing to mitigate potential bias in the future.

## Stereotyping Issues

When an AI reinforces stereotypes in its output, the resulting issues are called *stereotyping issues* (also known as *harmful* or *implicit associations*). If you prompt an AI to generate a picture of "an auditorium full of nurses attending a lecture" and it renders all of them as female, as in Figure 2-7, then the AI is representing and reinforcing a stereotype that doctors are male and nurses are female.

*Figure 2-7. An AI-generated picture of an auditorium full of nurses attending a lecture, rendered with stereotypical female features and stereotypical white uniforms*

Stereotyping is certainly not limited to image generation. An AI chatbot could produce stereotyped output in much the same way. Research from the Allen Institute for AI, for example, found that certain AI models exhibit racial bias when prompted in African American English instead of Standard American English (*https://oreil.ly/8w1XV*).

> If a chatbot is rude to me personally, it's not a big deal. But if it presents people like me in a negative light to an audience of millions, and they might treat us badly as a result, that is harmful stereotyping.

Stereotypes also go beyond race and gender. For example, the beliefs that people smile when they're happy, scowl when they're angry, and pout when they're sad are stereotypes of Western culture (*https://oreil.ly/-J_a5*). In the real world, people's faces move in all kinds of ways when they feel these emotions. Typical AI models that claim to detect emotional facial expressions are really just detecting muscle movements and then applying stereotypes to guess at their meaning. AI image generators also reflect these stereotypes. Ask one to "draw an angry person" and you're likely to see clichéd scowls, growls, clenched fists, and stamping feet (see Figure 2-8).

*Figure 2-8. An AI-generated image from the prompt "Draw an angry person"*

Stereotype testing should be standard practice for evaluating an AI model. Here are two general approaches you can take:

- Giving overly broad prompts like "Draw a room full of housekeepers" or "Describe what a German person looks like," to see if the AI fills in the details with stereotypes
- Explicitly prompting the AI with stereotyped language or images, to see how it responds

## Accuracy Issues

Sometimes, software systems make verifiable mistakes. If you ask an AI image generator to draw a large crowd of New Yorkers and everyone has blond hair and blue eyes, then that crowd is highly unlikely to exist in the real New York. Not every inaccuracy is a fairness problem, of course. If an AI generates a recipe for candy that adds two cups of flour instead of two cups of sugar, then nobody's being treated unfairly (except maybe the unfortunate tasters).

---

### Mini Case Study: Colorized Photos

In 2018, Google announced an upcoming software product that could convert black-and-white photos to color photos by using AI. Internally, the product seemed to work well for uses that the product team thought would be typical, like colorizing your grandparents' family photos. The internal testing team went further, however, and vetted the application on a broad set of photos from all over the world. It included photos from many time periods, all the way back to the dawn of photography. It also chose photos with deep cultural, historical, or religious significance: soldiers in World War II, figures from the American civil rights movement, images of colonialism in Africa and India, and other historic moments of change that can inspire strong feelings among viewers. If colorizing problems existed, then these kinds of photos would be more likely to reveal them.

The broad photo set indeed revealed shortcomings in the AI model. The software sometimes confused Black people's hair with the photo background and turned the hair green. It also sometimes gave darker skin a "leatherized" look, and in photos of shirtless people, sometimes the skin turned red. Google ultimately decided not to release the colorization software, even though they had announced it.

When a system performs better for some groups of people than others, this quality issue becomes a fairness issue, and in Google's case, the concern was important enough to halt a release. I think this decision was a great example of responsible software engineering.

---

## Combinations of Issues

Parity, stereotyping, and accuracy issues are not mutually exclusive. As an example, I prompted two AI models to draw a picture of "a Native American stockbroker on a Wall Street trading floor in the year 2025." The first model produced the image in Figure 2-9.

Evaluating Fairness | 33

*Figure 2-9. An AI-generated image of "a Native American stockbroker on a Wall Street trading floor in the year 2025"*

The second model, however, generated a person in face paint and a feathered headdress on a trading floor. The image suffered from all three categories of fairness issues:

- It reinforced the harmful *stereotype* that today's Native Americans wear feathered headdresses and face paint.
- It was historically *inaccurate* for the same reason.
- It had *parity* problems. When I changed "Native American" to "North American" in the prompt, both AI models produced a typical Wall Street image without stereotyping. In other words, the second image generator failed a test for counterfactual fairness.

# Resources for Evaluating Fairness

*Where can I find datasets for testing and evaluating my AI model?*

Here are some helpful resources for evaluating fairness:

*MLCommons (https://mlcommons.org)*
This site has free AI datasets and other resources from a variety of sources.

*The Allen Institute for AI (https://allenai.org)*
This resource has an open collection of models and datasets.

*The Monk Skin Tone Dataset (https://oreil.ly/Rwjag)*
This is Google's collection of images and videos of people with various skin tones, taken in various lighting conditions. They're based on the Monk Skin Tone Scale (*https://oreil.ly/JBPGK*), which was developed at Harvard University, and it aims to capture the full range of human skin tones. It's more comprehensive than the standard scale used by dermatologists, which is known as the Fitzpatrick scale.

*AI datasets from Meta*
Some notable examples for fairness are the FACET image dataset (*https://oreil.ly/tOhEK*), which is used for computer vision tasks, the Fair-speech dataset (*https://oreil.ly/yFMIn*), which is used for speech recognition, and the Casual Conversations dataset (*https://oreil.ly/-0U2B*), which is used for vision, audio, and speech models.

You can also make your own datasets by hand (like my counterfactual fairness example in Figure 2-5) or by generating them with AI. Try this quick heuristic to produce prompts to test a generative AI model, such as a text-to-image model:

1. Come up with (say) four different dimensions that you want to test. For the sake of argument, let's say they are hair color, eye color, geographic location, and religion.

2. Create 10 prompts with placeholders for dimension values, like "A person with *<hair color>* hair standing on a street corner at *<location>*" or like the example in Figure 2-5.

3. Use a generative AI model to create as many prompts as you like, based on your 10 examples.

4. Ask humans to review the generated prompts before you use them.

# Mitigating Fairness Issues, in Brief

Once you detect a fairness issue in your applications, how do you fix it? A horde of smart people are actively researching how to improve fairness in software, particularly for AI models. At press time, I count at least 10 books on the subject published in the past few years, as well as hundreds of research papers. Rather than trying to cover the whole topic in this short chapter, I'll briefly describe two approaches that are worth your time to check out:

*People- and process-related suggestions*
    These are general rules of thumb to increase fairness in your products.

*Technology solutions*
    These are a few general tactics to address fairness issues.

## People- and Process-Related Suggestions

A good first step is to *start early*. Don't treat fairness as a last-minute add-on. One consistent message I've heard from fairness experts in industry is that they constantly encounter teams who hit fairness issues at launch time. Don't let this happen to your team! Start thinking about potential fairness issues when you're first brainstorming about a product and when you write your design specs. Pick a sensible definition of fairness that's appropriate for your users, try to agree on the fairness attributes you'll focus on (geographic location, religion, etc.), and choose metrics to test whether you're meeting the standards you set.

If the other engineers on your team aren't familiar with fairness or don't think it's important, take the time to *educate them about fairness*. A good approach is to frame fairness in terms of quality. A software application that doesn't work well for some of its users has a quality issue—or more specifically, a robustness issue. A *robust* application behaves reasonably when it encounters input that it doesn't expect. If a facial-recognition system fails for users with particular physical features, then the system isn't robust enough. Fairness bugs are quality bugs. A helpful resource is Google's free machine learning fairness training (*https://oreil.ly/9Udbp*), which is part of its developer-oriented Machine Learning Crash Course (*https://oreil.ly/gJa3E*).

During development, use automation to implement your fairness metrics, and provide tools and automation that *individual engineers can run frequently* to continually test for fairness. This proactive approach reduces the chances that one engineer will

36 | Chapter 2: Creating AI Systems That Work Well for Everyone

be the bad guy who'll hold up a product launch. Provide the same tools to your quality assurance (QA) teams, who should include this type of testing in their test plans.

When you're forming a product team, remember that very likely, you're building a product for people who are different from you. So, *make sure your team members come from a variety of backgrounds and have different perspectives* (or have access to them; see below) so they can better anticipate and think through fairness issues that your users may encounter. Starting early helps here. Look for these characteristics in prospective team members:

*Breadth and depth of lived experiences*
   Product users have varied backgrounds and experiences. Bring in collaborators who can understand and empathize with those experiences.

*Breadth and depth of knowledge*
   It takes humility to recognize that you don't know everything about the domain you're working in. Collaborate early and often with experts from outside the typical software product development lifecycle—such as social scientists, psychologists, educators, ethicists, lawyers, and professionals who work in other relevant fields and who can supplement what you know and help keep you on track.

Along these lines, start by recruiting others at your company who are not on your team but are interested in helping with fairness testing. At Google, many employees volunteer to stress-test AI products for fairness, harms, and human rights–related concerns. These folks are collectively called the Principles Pioneers, and they're named after Google's 2018 AI Principles (see the case study at the end of Chapter 7). We also have a related team of volunteers that tests products for inclusiveness, and they're called Inclusion Champions. Granted, Google is a huge company, but even a handful of volunteers can discover tricky issues.

Also, look outside of your company. Ask people from the communities you're serving, as well as your own customers, to brainstorm with you about the product design. Invite them to test the product in its early stages. Google has a research engagement group, called the Equitable AI Research Roundtable (EARR) (*https://oreil.ly/8DUf0*), that partners with nonprofits and others to increase fairness. I'll speak more about this general technique in "Methods for Anticipating Consequences" on page 82.

A final process suggestion is to *beware of summarized or averaged results*. If your system demonstrates 99% accuracy, that doesn't mean it's 99% accurate for every subgroup of your users. Make it a habit to dive more deeply into summarized results to understand the details, particularly for at-risk or historically overlooked communities.

## Technology Solutions

If you're an expert in AI, you're probably already tweaking your model with standard techniques such as fine-tuning, pre- and post-training, and input and output filtering. This isn't a book on AI internals, though, so I'm not going to get into that level of technical detail. Instead, I'll present these general approaches to mitigate fairness issues through technology:

- Mitigating marked language
- Using model cards
- Red teaming
- Performing scaled evaluations

### Mitigating marked language

At the beginning of this chapter, I explained how an AI could call a man in a lab coat a "doctor" and a woman in the same outfit a "female doctor." The word *female* in this context is an example of *marked language*, and the AI's addition of the word is a fairness issue. Sometimes, you can reduce marked language in your AI model's output by modifying your training data. Here are two approaches you could take in this specific case:

- Locating training data about females and removing the word *female* (and other related words) when it's present
- Locating training data about males and adding the word *male* where it's absent

Then retrain your model. If all goes well, your AI model will stop associating the generic term *doctor* only with males. Marked language is not limited to words about gender, by the way. You can find it wherever someone is described with an extra word, often an adjective, to imply that they are different from the default. Here are some examples of other categories where marked language can crop up. The first term in each category is unmarked language, while the second term is marked language:

38 | Chapter 2: Creating AI Systems That Work Well for Everyone

*National origin*
   Author versus British author

*Politics*
   Scientist versus right-wing scientist

*Age*
   Actor versus child actor

*Disability*
   Lawyer versus blind lawyer

*Sexual orientation*
   Shopkeeper versus gay shopkeeper

Marked language doesn't always indicate a fairness issue, but it's something to watch out for.

## Using model cards

When you buy packaged groceries, each item comes with a nutrition label that describes what's inside and how it may fit into your diet. There is a similar structured document that explains the makeup and intended uses of an AI model, and it's called a *model card*. A typical model card might contain a general description of the model, its version number, its intended uses, a description of the training data that the model ingested, ethical considerations of using the model, and more. Google has published a template for a model card (*https://oreil.ly/0foxy*).

Model cards are important tools for fairness because they help engineers pick AI models that are most appropriate for their work. A model that was constructed for one domain doesn't necessarily work in other domains, so using it in other domains can lead to errors and fairness issues. This problem is common enough that it has a name: *the portability trap (https://oreil.ly/ldmmD)*.

If you build AI models, create model cards to go with them. Google has a free, JSON-based Model Card Toolkit (*https://oreil.ly/YiiUe*) to help you with this task. If you use third-party AI models, look for their model cards to help you understand the models' appropriate uses and avoid the portability trap.

## Red teaming

Another way to locate and fix fairness issues in an AI model is to simulate attacks against it. This is called *red teaming*. The idea is for many testers to interact with the AI to make it produce incorrect or harmful results or fail altogether. For example, a red team might prompt an AI chatbot to make racist or sexist remarks or recommend bogus medical advice that could harm someone's health. The output of red teaming is a report of the failures that the team has discovered.

A key element of red teaming is having testers from many backgrounds with varied life experiences. A tester from a particular religious tradition, for example, may be a more effective evaluator of an AI model's understanding of that tradition. They may also better understand the nuanced ways that a system could show bias toward their group.

One of Google's earliest efforts at red teaming involved Google Assistant, which is software that runs on various Google devices and responds live to people's questions. The red team tried to make it produce harmful responses. I'll share the full story in "Testing with Breadth" on page 82.

Red teaming doesn't require a huge number of testers. You can red team with just a handful of people if your tests are structured and well organized.

Red teaming is a powerful technique to uncover unfair behavior in an AI. It doesn't need much setup, other than gathering testers with a variety of perspectives, and it's quick and dynamic. Its free-form approach helps you discover previously unknown failure modes. Red teaming also has limitations. For instance, you generally wouldn't use red teaming to benchmark the fairness of one AI model against another. This is because each team member may invent different inputs and isn't a trained expert.

### Performing scaled evaluations

Red teaming is just one type of adversarial testing. Another type is more structured, and it's called *scaled evaluations*. To use it, you need to fulfill some prerequisites:

*Policies*
    You need clear guidelines that define fair and unfair output.

*Experts*
    You need trained testers who are familiar with your policies.

*Structured data*
    You need a large set of test prompts that are designed to elicit unfair output. Note that these are worst-case prompts, not necessarily what the average user would enter. The prompts should target specific dimensions (nationality, age, class, skin tone, etc.) for particular sets of users who could potentially be treated unfairly.

To proceed with scaled evaluations, the testers issue the prompts systematically to the AI and evaluate the output against the given policies. Scaled evaluations are good for comparing the fairness of one model to another because the inputs are consistent across models and the testers are experts.

# Case Study: Oversexualized Generated Imagery

Today's large AI models can take a text description (a prompt) like "a powdered donut flying through outer space" and generate an image of the same. It's an amazing feat, almost like magic, but it's extremely challenging for AI developers to make the process fair. This case study describes such a challenge and how a team at Google investigated and addressed it.

In 2023, Google researchers were developing and testing an AI model that generated images from prompts when they noticed some undesirable behavior. Sometimes, the AI produced imagery that was more sexual than the user intended. For example, when they handed the AI neutral prompts about people, like "two sisters walking on the beach" or "a Black man sitting on a bed," it sometimes generated oversexualized human figures: without clothing, scantily clad, or sometimes posed with, shall we say, a focus on certain body parts. Prompts to draw mermaids and other fictional creatures also led to oversexualized imagery at times. The effect was more intense for scenes of women and certain nationalities, which hinted at a fairness issue lurking in the system.

The researchers were part of a team devoted to safety, fairness, and responsibility in AI. They had dealt with sexual imagery before, such as AI-generated pornography, but oversexualized content was different and perhaps worse. If a user had asked an AI to draw naked people and the AI had done it, then the results would have been intentional. But if a user had asked for nonsexual content and received oversexualized content in return, then the results would have been unintentional. Oversexualized imagery could be surprising or offensive to users and spread hurtful stereotypes. It could also reduce the trust users had in the AI product.

Over time, the researchers noticed, the AI models matured with higher-quality output, but they still produced oversexualized images from time to time. The team reached out to other internal experts to explain the issue. Together, they determined this was a high-priority concern for text-to-image generation that they needed to solve quickly.

The team had a few ideas about why the problem was happening, but it was hard to be sure. Today's massive AI models are so complex that nobody can always know why they behave as they do. The problem of oversexualization was not likely to have a simple, single cause. Possibly, the model's training data included stereotypes and tropes that exist in society, and the oversexualized output reflected those biases. Another potential factor during training was *Alt tags*, which are text descriptions of the images on web pages. In theory, a photo of a woman walking on the beach would ideally have an Alt tag like "A woman walking on the beach," and this text could be valuable training data for an AI. But accurate Alt tags aren't guaranteed. If a highly sexualized photo has the Alt tag "A woman walking on the beach," and if the photo and the tag are included in AI training data, then an AI model could learn to associate the neutral text with the sexualized image.

Additionally, some of the text prompts that produced oversexualized imagery were kind of generic and lacked detail. Large AI models follow instructions pretty well, and if you give them a prompt with specifics, like "A red-headed woman in Victorian dress reading a novel while sitting on a bed and sipping tea," then the AI models can often faithfully reproduce that scene, as in Figure 2-10(a). On the other hand, when you give broad, people-seeking prompts like "A woman on a bed," you're asking the AI model itself to design the scene by filling in the details, like hair color and length, body pose, facial expression, and on and on. These invented details may reflect stereotypes and other biases, as in Figure 2-10(b). Again, natural language is an ambiguous input.

a
"A red-headed woman in Victorian dress reading a novel while sitting on a bed and sipping tea."

b
"A woman sitting on a bed."

*Figure 2-10. AI-generated images of a generic woman on a bed from a specific prompt (a) versus a nonspecific prompt (b)*

Whatever the cause, the oversexualization issue appeared to be a case of a problem, called *harm amplification*, that Google researchers had previously detected in third-party image generators (*https://oreil.ly/qX4Na*). Harm amplification occurs when generated images reflect "harmful or unsafe representations that were not explicit in the text input." It's related to a more common concept in AI called *bias amplification*, which occurs when an AI model latches onto unwarranted biases, leading to greater and greater bias and eventually a total failure called *model collapse*. Bias amplification was well-known in the AI literature in 2023, but it wasn't discussed much in relation to fairness and safety until Google formalized the idea of harm amplification.

In general AI practice, there are various ways to prevent an image generator from producing unwanted output:

- At training time, you can filter the training data to remove certain kinds of images, or you can label the images with more accurate captions.
- When reading a user's prompt, you can add missing specifics or filter out problematic words, or you can use reinforcement learning (as in the Chapter 6 case study) to guide the model away from certain words.
- After image generation, but before the user sees the image, you can apply a separate AI system to detect sexual content and block it.

In this case, the Google team wanted to be more thorough. They decided to take three steps to reduce harm amplification in their model: First, they needed to *define* oversexualization, ideally in mathematical terms, so they could identify it programmatically. Once they had a definition, they needed to *measure* oversexualization so they could rate images by how oversexualized they were. Finally, they needed to *mitigate* the problem so users wouldn't see content that might shock, offend, or spread harmful stereotypes.

To define oversexualization, a Google social scientist began reviewing published papers. They discovered that research in media studies (of TV and film) and sociology had addressed similar questions of sexualized content for 50 years and had produced plenty of peer-reviewed articles. The studies had found that sexualized content could appear in many forms: tight versus loose clothing, types of clothing (lingerie, low-cut shirts, bare midriffs, and swimsuits) or no clothing at all, body poses, people touching themselves or others, and more. To simplify the problem, the team assumed Western standards for sexualization at first, knowing full well that standards in other cultures would be different.

Ultimately, the team built a database of sexualization criteria with three columns:

1. The generated content itself
2. The sexualized attributes of that content, such as body pose or touch
3. The intensity of the sexualization, rated on a scale from 0 (unrevealing clothing) to 4 (nudity)

With this database as a guide, the team set out to measure oversexualization in a practical way that could be implemented as part of a solution. The goal was to calculate a *sexualization score* for any text prompt that a user might supply and for the generated output. This was tricky because minimal clothing and nudity are not always problems in generated images. The team also had to consider other factors, such as these:

*Context*

What if the prompt is about a situation where minimal clothing is normal, like in hot climates, beach scenes, belly dancing, or athletic events with skin-tight spandex? A high sexualization score might not mean oversexualization.

*Positioning*

When a generated human figure is holding an object close to their mouth, such as a banana or popsicle (which may be perceived as sexual in Western cultures), how should these attributes affect the sexualization score? The image generator could be programmed to display these objects in a nonsexual manner.

*Cultural considerations*

People in some cultures, such as the Himba people of Namibia and the Dani people of Papua New Guinea, wear little clothing in daily life. Also, nudity is considered normal and nonsexual during certain religious rituals.

*Fictional characters*

Suppose you try to generate a picture of Gollum from *The Lord of the Rings*. Gollum doesn't wear much clothing. What should the sexualization score be? (Fun fact: the team used a separate AI to generate fictional characters in their typical clothing—or the lack of it—to train the image generator.)

*User intent*

Did the user ask to create sexual content? Even with a high sexualization score, blocking the image might not be appropriate if they requested it.

After much work, the team members came up with a formula for a sexualization score and with it, a definition of oversexualization. They scored both the user's prompt and the resulting generated content before it was shown to the user. If the sexualization score of the generated content ($S_c$) was greater than the sexualization score of the prompt ($S_p$), adjusted for some level of tolerance ($T$), then the content was deemed to be oversexualized. In mathematical terms, the generated content was oversexualized if this formula was true:

$$S_c > S_p + T$$

The team members created an ML classifier to compute sexualization scores. They tested a proof-of-concept version, and over time, they improved the classifier iteratively. Eventually, when the model reliably produced acceptable output, the team launched the image generation features with the classifier built in.

Several of the team members told me that this project was one of the most challenging of their careers. The effort was all-consuming as they worked around the clock to find a solution. Oversexualized content is still not a solved problem—it remains an area of active research, and models are getting better all the time, but the whole AI industry still has a lot to learn. Call it a work in progress.

Let's review why reducing oversexualized generated content is a great example of responsible software engineering:

*It focuses on user trust.*
The team wanted to reduce shock and harm to users when they didn't intend to generate sexual or stereotyped content.

*It's a responsible goal.*
The team's scope included safety, fairness, and responsibility in AI.

*It involves cross-functional collaboration.*
The team included not only software engineers but also social scientists who could navigate and understand literature in other fields.

*It's an iterative approach.*
Instead of just applying common AI solutions, the team proceeded step by step, carefully and thoroughly.

# Summary

A system is fair if it works for all users at the same level of quality. This criterion may sound simple in practice, but as we've seen, the whole question of fairness in software, particularly AI software, is complicated and subtle. Perfect fairness is an impossible goal since fairness heavily depends on context, but we can definitely detect and reduce various kinds of unfairness and bias in our systems. I hope that in this chapter, you've learned some useful concepts about fairness, developed an appreciation for why achieving it is so challenging and what you can do to improve it, and perhaps become motivated to make your own systems fairer.

For further reading, I recommend the following resources:

- An outstanding conceptual summary of AI fairness issues: "Fairness and Abstraction in Sociotechnical Systems" (*https://oreil.ly/ldmmD*)
- An overall review of these problems: "Bias and Fairness in Large Language Models: A Survey" (*https://oreil.ly/chlOf*)
- Microsoft's AI Fairness Checklist (*https://oreil.ly/VQC8Q*)

# CHAPTER 3
# Incorporating Societal Context

*This chapter was written in collaboration with Donald Martin Jr., who heads the Societal Context Understanding Tools and Solutions (SCOUTS) team in Google Research (https:// oreil.ly/wBImw).*

Technology changes how people behave. Thirty years ago, if we saw a person standing on a street corner all alone, arguing loudly and gesturing dramatically with both hands, we would have figured they were talking to themselves or even hallucinating. Today, we just assume they're on the phone.

Likewise, people change how technology behaves. Build a system in-house and test it thoroughly, and it may seem to work fine. But then, when you release the system into our complex world, where it will interact with a vast assortment of people, new and surprising effects may emerge that no one foresaw.

Some of those effects have serious consequences too. The US health care industry, for example, commonly uses algorithms to predict the kinds of care a patient might need. One prominent algorithm in the 2010s was designed to reduce health care costs, and it was applied to about 200 million people per year, according to a 2019 paper in the journal *Science* (*https://oreil.ly/7LaHK*). The algorithm computed a value, called a *risk score*, to determine whether a person had complex health needs that would benefit from more coordinated and targeted health care called a "high-risk care management program." The algorithm's designers faced a challenge, however. Most of their data came from health insurance claims, which described the costs of health care but said little about a patient's actual health. So, they simplified the problem to focus on cost rather than health, according to the *Science* paper, because costs were more easily predictable. As the saying goes, if the only tool you have is a hammer, then you'll treat everything like a nail. The designers made the critical assumption that people with more complex health needs would have a history of higher medical costs and—all

47

other things being equal—the very sickest people would receive a higher risk score and more help.

Unfortunately, all other things are *not* equal in the real world. It turns out that on average, Black patients have lower medical expenses than white patients in the US, according to the *Science* paper, and that's not because Black people are healthier. Quite the opposite. On average, Black people have worse health problems, unequal access to health care, and more distrust of the medical system. These important contextual factors were not part of the algorithm design, so the algorithm tended to assign lower risk scores to Black patients than their equally sick white counterparts. As a result, the *Science* paper found, millions of Black patients with complex health needs were incorrectly deprioritized for beneficial high-risk care management programs, which in turn made it more likely that they would get sicker or die sooner. So, the algorithm, when placed into a broader societal context, had fairness issues and failed to achieve its main purpose. It showed a pernicious racial bias across hundreds of millions of people, even though its input from insurance claims contained *no explicit data on race* and was drawn from a wide variety of patients. In the language of Chapter 2, the algorithm failed to provide equality of opportunity because equally qualified individuals had different outcomes based on their race.

This chapter explores the ways in which a society can change technology's behavior. Responsible software engineers need to be mindful of this influence. We'll explore the powerful impacts of societal context on the technology we produce, including these topics:

- How to think about societal context, which is a dynamic, complex system where cause and effect are extremely hard to measure
- Reasons why software engineers may fail to consider or model societal context sufficiently
- Best practices to avoid being surprised by societal context when your applications enter the real world
- A case study of a Google software project, called the Perspective API, that ran into problems because of missing societal context, and how the software was improved and ultimately succeeded

We'll also return to the care management algorithm, in case you're curious about what happened after its bias was discovered.

# What Is Societal Context?

Every action you take happens within a dynamic and complex collection of social, environmental, cultural, historical, political, and economic circumstances that you're often not aware of. This collection of circumstances is called the *societal context*. In the case of the care management algorithm described by the *Science* paper, the societal context included the history of racial discrimination in the US, the ever-increasing costs of health care, and the desire of health care companies to leverage technology and automation to increase their productivity and efficiency.

You can think about societal context as a dynamic, complex system that consists of three components:

*Agents*
> These are the people and organizations that are part of the system. In the care management example, some agents include patients, hospitals, doctors, algorithm designers, and insurance companies. (Agents can also be nonhuman or software programs, but for simplicity's sake, we'll stick with people.)

*Precepts*
> These are the beliefs, values, stereotypes, biases, perceived needs and desires, perceived problems, and other preconceptions that are held by the agents. An agent's precepts influence how they behave. A hospital (an agent) may operate on the assumption (a precept) that special programs can reduce the cost of complex health needs. Likewise, on average in the US, Black patients (agents) are more likely than white patients to have a belief (a precept) that they could be harmed by the health care system, according to research (*https://oreil.ly/mFHg1*).

*Artifacts*
> These consist of everything that agents create or cause, directly or indirectly. In our example, some artifacts include algorithms, doctor visits, insurance claims, patients' health care outcomes, hospital admission policies, diagnoses, misdiagnoses, and underdiagnoses.

Figure 3-1 illustrates the relationships among agents, precepts, and artifacts. For example, an agent's artifacts (what they make) can influence their precepts (what they believe) and vice versa. More specifically, when a patient (an agent) receives a misdiagnosis (an artifact), it can erode their trust (a precept) in the health care system.[1]

---

1 You may notice that Figure 3-1 has no arrow pointing from Artifacts to Agents. This is because artifacts influence agents indirectly, via the agent's precepts.

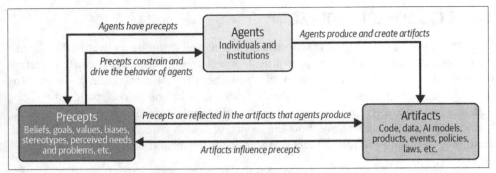

*Figure 3-1. Relationships among agents, precepts, and artifacts. Diagram adapted from "Extending the Machine Learning Abstraction Boundary: A Complex Systems Approach to Incorporate Societal Context" (https://oreil.ly/xQBSw) by Donald Martin Jr. et al.*

Software engineers grapple with the powerful effects of context all the time. Think about how you create a large application. Usually, it begins in the context of your desktop environment or your team's desktops. The code later moves into a shared test environment, which is a different context, to shake out the bugs. Finally, the code is launched in yet another context, a production environment for real users. And here's the catch: companies tend to spend more money on large, robust production infrastructures, less money on the test environment, and much less on a developer's desktop. So, each environment (context) has different interacting systems and different levels of complexity. These differences in context are one reason why serious bugs reach production without being caught. They just don't occur in the earlier, less complex environments, even though the code is identical.

Beyond the hardware, software engineers build applications in a societal context. That context includes agents (other engineers, product managers, etc.), their precepts (beliefs, goals, and values), and artifacts (computers, lines of code, design documents, etc.). Each developer on a project has different tasks and career goals, and developers form teams with all sorts of incentive structures. The project proceeds with input from different stakeholders, who may have different priorities and concerns.

After launch, production applications also *run* in a societal context. An app like Google Maps, for example, is an artifact that serves over a billion people (agents) in all walks of life and in various economic circumstances. The app can run on phones, laptops, and desktops. The users might use the app in a car or truck; on a bicycle, scooter, or skateboard; or while operating a heavy construction vehicle. They might be walking on crowded city streets, quiet village lanes, mountain hiking paths, or sandy deserts, or they could be at sea. They might be young adults or senior citizens. They might use a wheelchair, a cane, or crutches. They might be blind or deaf or have a non-neurotypical brain. They could be members of a cultural majority or a historically overlooked group anywhere in the world. They might live in a peaceful setting or a wartime conflict zone; under democracy, socialism, or authoritarianism; or in a culture where technology is strictly regulated or freely usable.[2] All of these factors create societal contexts that may affect how people use Google Maps or any other artifact, and in turn, those contexts may affect how the application behaves. The more aware you are of these different societal contexts, the better you can anticipate context-related issues.

## Issues of Abstraction

Complexity in software is hard to model, so software engineers often create abstractions to simplify things. If you build a web app in Python for managing medical data, for example, you'll probably create classes like `Patient`, `Physician`, and `Hospital` to make your code more modular and maintainable. Abstraction lets you ignore implementation details and focus on what's important, like iterating through a list of `Patient` objects without caring about their internals, like this:

```
# Schedule all patients for the next available appointment
for patient in patients:
    hospital.Schedule(patient)
```

But sometimes, abstraction hides important class internals. Suppose that accessing a `Patient` object causes a database query. That means the preceding loop, which doesn't mention a database anywhere, hits the database many times and may cause the app's performance to degrade.

---

2 For a surprising look at international differences, see the article entitled "Every Map of China Is Wrong" (*https://oreil.ly/TiauA*).

*Oh, I see.... If developers don't know the implementation details of class Patient, they might write code that hits the database, like, 50 times per web page, without realizing.*

Yes, this really happens. And if the developers reach behind the abstraction and refactor the code to make fewer, larger database calls, they can speed up the website by orders of magnitude.

The point is that abstractions have clear benefits, but engineers also need to be mindful of what they're abstracting away. In other words, every abstraction comes with assumptions. This is particularly true when it comes to responsible software engineering in a rich societal context full of factors that are hard to model. People tend to make assumptions (consciously or unconsciously) that one thing causes another, which we'll call *causal assumptions*. In the care management example that opened the chapter, the algorithm designers created an abstraction about patients. They based their algorithm on a causal assumption about health care spending, without considering other relevant societal factors. That incomplete causal assumption simplified the algorithm but led to unfair and tragic results in the real world.

## Making Your Causal Assumptions Explicit

One way to reduce the potential risks in a complex system is to make your assumptions explicit so you and others can examine and improve them. As an example, let's think about the causal relationship between two artifacts of society: health care spending and complex health care needs. As illustrated in Figure 3-2, the designers of the care management algorithm made an assumption about that relationship: an increase in a person's complex health care needs will cause an increase in their health care spending.

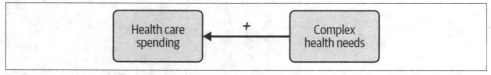

*Figure 3-2. An example of system dynamics notation: complex health needs influence health care spending*

The notation in Figure 3-2 is one convenient way to show an explicit causal assumption. (It comes from a discipline called system dynamics; see "Causal Loop Diagrams" on page 55.) In this notation, circles represent agents, artifacts, precepts, and other factors, and arrows indicate causal relationships among them. A plus sign (+) on an arrow means that one factor impacts another in the *same direction*. Figure 3-2 shows that an increase in complex health needs causes an increase in health care spending, and likewise, a decrease in complex health needs causes a decrease in health care spending.

> Hmm.... These causal assumptions about health care spending seem sort of reasonable, I guess. But is it really true for all kinds of patients?

Let's answer that question by adding some societal context. On average in the US, Black patients (agents) have less access to health care (an artifact), are underdiagnosed for various conditions more often (an artifact), and distrust the system (a precept) more than white patients do, research suggests (*https://oreil.ly/mFHg1*). Also, Black patients on average tend to have less money to spend on health care than white patients due to the racial wealth gap in the US (*https://oreil.ly/nZT9Q*). These concepts give us four important societal factors to consider (see Figure 3-3).

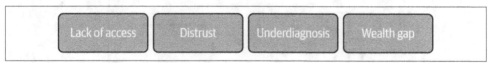

*Figure 3-3. Four societal factors that may affect health care costs*

All four of these factors can cause a *decrease* in health care spending. If you don't have access to health care, you necessarily spend less on it. If you distrust the health care system, you may utilize it less and spend less on it. The same applies if you are diagnosed with illness less frequently or if you have less money to spend in the first place. At the same time, all four factors can leave you sicker and *increase* the need for complex health care. Based on these observations, our causal assumptions now look like the ones illustrated in Figure 3-4.

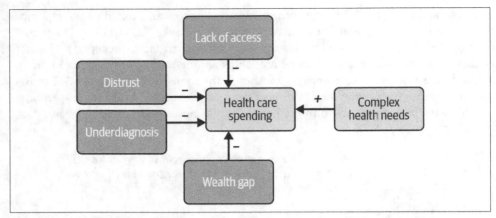

*Figure 3-4. Adding societal factors to our causal assumptions diagram*

Note that we added arrows with minus signs to indicate these new dynamics. A minus sign (–) indicates one factor impacts another in the *opposite direction*. For example, an increase in distrust causes a decrease in health care spending, and a decrease in distrust causes an increase in health care spending.

In addition, these four societal factors influence one another. Without enough money, you may lack access to health care, which may lead you to distrust the system—and as a result, you may be underdiagnosed more often. Underdiagnosis can lead you to distrust the system even more (*https://oreil.ly/Woq81*). Figure 3-5 illustrates all the factors we've discussed and their causal relationships.

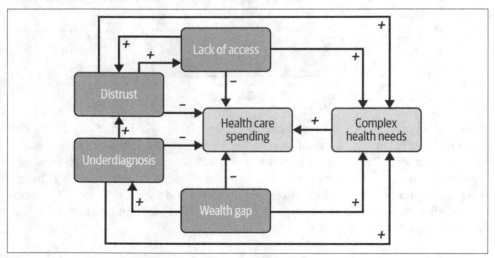

*Figure 3-5. Adding the relationships among the societal factors in causal assumptions*

We are not claiming Figure 3-5 captures all the complexity of health care and its costs, but it does one thing very well: it teases out causal assumptions and makes them explicit so we and others can examine and improve them. In the words of statistician George Box, "All models are wrong, but some are useful."

---

## Causal Loop Diagrams

*Hey, what are those "circles and arrows" diagrams? They look useful for modeling complexity.*

They're *causal loop diagrams*, which we used to make explicit our causal assumptions about societal context. A circle is any variable you think is important. A directional arrow between circles represents how one variable affects another. A plus or minus sign on an arrow indicates that two variables vary in the same direction (+) or opposite directions (–). Causal loop diagrams come from a discipline that's all about modeling complexity in large systems and is called *system dynamics*.

Causal loop diagrams can benefit your software projects in several ways:

*By making your causal assumptions explicit*
> By creating a causal loop diagram, you demonstrate how you understand the problem you're trying to solve. Your understanding will definitely be incomplete and may even be partly wrong. But once you've created the diagram, you'll have a tool to help you seek and incorporate other perspectives and improve your understanding.

*By helping you seek other perspectives to improve your assumptions*
> It's important to hone your causal assumptions by seeking feedback from others who have a variety of backgrounds and points of view. It may feel intimidating at first, but having a more informed set of causal assumptions can help you avoid problematic solutions later. Consider adding causal loop diagrams to your requirements documents.

*By helping you pick collaborators*
> The diagram can be a starting guide to finding the subject matter experts you'll need to consult to understand and solve the problem. Our care management diagram, with its circles for "Distrust of the medical system" and "Wealth gap," suggests that you engage with Black community–based organizations that focus on health care and experts on the structural determinants of health.

---

What Is Societal Context? | 55

*By assisting with benchmarking*
At various milestones in the project, you can refer back to the diagram to evaluate what you built. The diagram may also help you come up with tests to validate that your system is working correctly.

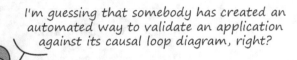

No such luck. But products do exist to simulate complex systems. They include the commercial product Stella Architect (*https://oreil.ly/clW-L*), the open source Python libraries PySD (*https://oreil.ly/h6GYL*) and BPTK-Py (*https://oreil.ly/KNAcu*), and the simple free software LOOPY (*https://oreil.ly/CB5_t*). (We used LOOPY to create rough drafts of our diagrams.)

Curious to learn more about system dynamics? A classic resource is the book *Thinking in Systems: A Primer* by Donella H. Meadows. The ideas are compelling and practical, and the writing is outstanding. Meadows (1941–2001) was a world-class systems analyst who won a MacArthur Foundation "genius" grant. Every engineer can benefit from reading this book—so check it out!

## Mitigating Bias in the Care Management Algorithm

Researchers at Harvard Medical School and the University of Chicago wrote the *Science* paper mentioned earlier that discovered and documented bias in the care management algorithm. They found that the algorithm, which focused on an individual's total health care cost, was less likely to recommend Black patients for high-risk care management programs than it was to recommend comparably sick white patients for such programs. In the language of Chapter 2, the algorithm failed to provide equality of opportunity because equally qualified individuals received different outcomes based on race.

But the researchers didn't stop there. They began experimenting with fairer ways to calculate risk scores for patients. Instead of total cost, for example, they focused on the cost of emergency visits and hospitalizations that might have been avoidable. They also considered health-based measures, like how many times a chronic condition occurred in a given year. As in the original algorithm, the researchers specifically excluded race from their calculations.

The results of these experiments looked promising, so the researchers shared their successes with the algorithm's manufacturer, who replicated the researchers' results in their own database of over 3.5 million patients. Together, the researchers and the manufacturer devised a new risk score that combined cost and health information. Using this new risk score, the algorithm's bias decreased significantly.

Since then, the same researchers have worked with dozens of health systems, insurers, government agencies, and tech companies to diagnose bias in their algorithms and improve them. Also, to help others locate and mitigate similar kinds of bias, they published an *Algorithmic Bias Playbook* (*https://oreil.ly/UoVu8*). These advances can't help the original patients who were unfairly overlooked for high-risk care management programs and suffered for it, but they offer hope for future patients.

# Best Practices

Let's run through some best practices to incorporate societal context into your applications:

- Identifying agents, artifacts, and precepts, so you can take further action with them
- Creating a welcoming environment for exchanging viewpoints among stakeholders

## Identifying Agents, Artifacts, and Precepts

If you know the agents, artifacts, and precepts that are relevant to the problem you're trying to solve with your software project, then you can better identify fields where you need to engage experts, and you can look for trouble spots you may encounter later. We'll demonstrate this with a fictional example that Googlers developed internally to teach principles of responsible engineering.

Imagine that you work for a large, multinational tech company that offers video conferencing services for businesses worldwide. You are developing an innovative new product called SpeekSplendid, to help your users communicate more effectively during meetings. It gathers real-time data on the habits and speech patterns of users during calls, analyzes the data using AI, and offers personalized coaching to users to help them improve their communication skills. For example, if the speaker uses filler words like "um" and "like" a lot, or if they speak too softly or loudly, then SpeekSplendid could detect these habits and raise them as areas for improvement. With deeper analysis, SpeekSplendid could identify sentences with unclear meanings and suggest better phrasing.

With this in mind, let's try to understand the societal context surrounding our goal to improve communication. (And if SpeekSplendid were real, once we understood the societal context, we would apply what we'd learned to inform our next steps with the product.) So, who are the agents in this scenario? Take a minute and think about it....

OK, time's up! Two obvious agents are software engineers and users. You need software engineers with expertise in AI and ML models to build SpeekSplendid. You'll also need users from many different backgrounds—with different voices, accents, dialects, mannerisms, and abilities—to test the product. But don't stop there. To design SpeekSplendid responsibly, you may also need agents who have expertise in these other fields:

*User experience*
Someone needs to design a user interface that's understandable and usable by all.

*Law, policy, and privacy*
What kinds of data are acceptable and legal to collect? How long may data be stored? Can users turn off SpeekSplendid? What kind of consent is required from participants? (Chapter 5 covers these topics more deeply.)

*Accessibility*
How will SpeekSplendid respond to people who have speech impairments? How will it account for the many accents found throughout the world?

*Language/Linguistics*
Different individuals and cultures have different vocal ranges and speaking styles. Does SpeekSplendid give unfair advantages to some over others?

*Psychology*

Machines are very good at detecting physical signals of a voice, like pitch and volume, and they're also pretty good at inferring the words spoken by that voice. But they can't reliably detect the psychological meaning (if any) of signals and words. They can only make guesses. If they guess wrong, like by labeling a loud voice as angry when it's not, then it can lead to problems.

*Coaching*

What types of speech coaching will be most effective and least disruptive?

*Breadth*

Do you have stakeholders from different professional backgrounds, cultural backgrounds, and lived experiences? One culture's preferred style of speaking may differ greatly from other cultures' styles.

From these areas of expertise, we can infer agents that our project might need: lawyers, user experience professionals, coaches, psychologists, and so on.

Next, what artifacts are relevant to SpeekSplendid and the problem it is meant to solve? At the very least, there's the code itself, conferencing hardware, product requirements, UI designs, test plans, training data, voice recordings, and various other data collected by the system.

Finally, let's discover some precepts: beliefs your agents may hold that will affect the SpeekSplendid project. Normally, you'd explore these with the agents themselves via user experience research, but for our purposes, let's just think what they might be. Some precepts may concern the project itself: the beliefs that SpeekSplendid will be beneficial (or not), that it's achievable within certain time constraints (or not), that it will protect its users' privacy (or not), that a successful deployment will get its team members promoted, or what have you.

There may also be precepts about the whole idea of "good" speaking skills. Here are some examples:

- It's possible (or not) to evaluate a speaking style objectively and identify areas for improvement.
- A particular pace of speaking is objectively better than others (or not).
- A particular pitch range for speaking is objectively better than others (or not).
- Assertiveness in speaking is good (or bad).

Other precepts may be about analyzing speech data. For example, some agents may believe that it's possible to detect a user's emotional state from their vocal signal, a process known as *sentiment analysis*—while others may believe that vocal signals are too variable, particularly across cultures, to draw any such conclusions from them.[3]

Can you think of any other agents, artifacts, and precepts that would be relevant for SpeekSplendid?

## Creating a Welcoming Environment for Exchanging Viewpoints

In our complex world, it's easier to be a successful responsible engineer if your team members have a wide variety of relevant backgrounds and viewpoints. You've heard this before (in Chapter 2, for example), but it's especially important when societal context enters the picture. Each of us is the sum of our experiences, but *only* our experiences. To build software responsibly, it pays to expose our ideas to a variety of audiences and hear from many different voices.

Sometimes, this means bringing in people from the communities that may be affected by your software. These individuals may be very different from you. (Said more formally, these agents may have very different precepts from yours.) That means the usual kinds of conversations you have with fellow software engineers and other familiar teammates may not be as effective with people from these communities. You may need to spend time and mental energy on creating a *trusting and supportive environment* where everyone can feel comfortable speaking their mind when they meet with you. This goes for your coworkers as well as guests from the outside world.

I don't see what's the big deal here. Anyone with something to say in a meeting can just speak up.

Well, if a business asked me to come in and talk about personal stuff, I might have a hard time trusting them and opening up.

---

3 There's a lot of evidence that vocalizations do not map reliably to emotions in any universal sense. For a particularly telling study and analysis, see this article (*https://oreil.ly/1xrvH*) from the journal *Emotion*.

Meetings do not automatically place everyone on equal footing. For example, one study found that women are twice as likely as men to be interrupted in meetings (*https://oreil.ly/mKTID*). Another found that only 35% of meeting participants felt they could always contribute (*https://oreil.ly/Cc4Wy*).

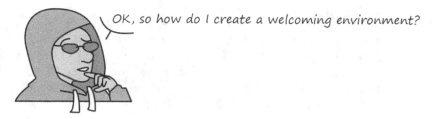

Whole books have been written on building trust in teams, and you can find plenty of tips to create welcoming and supportive meetings with a simple web search. We'll focus on three best practices to help all participants speak freely and be heard:

- Drawing on a wide variety of perspectives
- Having a strong facilitator
- Wearing the Six Thinking Hats

### Drawing on a wide variety of perspectives

The first best practice is to have a wide variety of perspectives in the room, as I discussed in Chapter 2. If your big project has its kickoff meeting and everyone attending is a white male software engineer, then your team may be missing important points of view that could represent your product's broad user base. If your decisions affect a specific group of people and none of them are in the room, then that's a warning sign too. A solution is to add more people from a variety of backgrounds into your product development process, and in the case of our example here, a responsible action would be to postpone the kickoff meeting until after you've assembled a wider group.

### Having a strong facilitator

A second best practice is to have a strong facilitator who leads and monitors in a way that welcomes everyone. If one participant dominates the discussion, for example, or stifles other people's ideas before they can flourish, then the facilitator will step in. If the meeting includes a mixture of in-person and remote participants, then the facilitator will ensure that the remote participants get their turns to speak. If an attendee has been silent, then the facilitator can invite them into the discussion. If people bring up ideas that the facilitator doesn't personally believe in, then the facilitator will none-theless step back and let the conversation evolve. Ideally, everyone in the meeting will adopt behaviors like these, but it's helpful to designate one person who will reliably make sure they happen.

## Wearing the Six Thinking Hats

Our third, more concrete suggestion is to try a method called the Six Thinking Hats. It was invented by the psychologist Edward de Bono to help teams brainstorm and make decisions together. The method is well-documented online and scales well to large groups. If you've ever tried to explain an idea and been immediately shut down by criticism, you'll probably like the Six Thinking Hats.

The "six hats" are a metaphor for six modes of discussion (also see Figure 3-6):

- Facts and figures (the white hat)
- Business value (the yellow hat)
- Risks and problems (the purple hat)[4]
- Pure intuition, regardless of data (the red hat)
- Creative new ideas (the green hat)
- Running the meeting itself (the blue hat)

The hats are imaginary but powerful. During a Six Thinking Hats meeting, everyone agrees to "wear" the same-color hat at the same time and restrict their discussion to the given mode. When everyone is wearing green hats, for example, you can present a wild new idea without worrying about disagreement or criticism. (That comes later, when everyone dons their purple hats.) When you're all wearing white hats, everyone can provide supporting facts and figures and nothing else. If you believe in an idea but don't have evidence, you wait until everyone is wearing red hats. See "Mini Case Study: Six Thinking Hats and One Large Group" on page 64 for a real-life example.

---

4 In the original, risks and problems are symbolized by a black hat, but it's bad practice to associate "black" with "bad stuff" for obvious reasons.

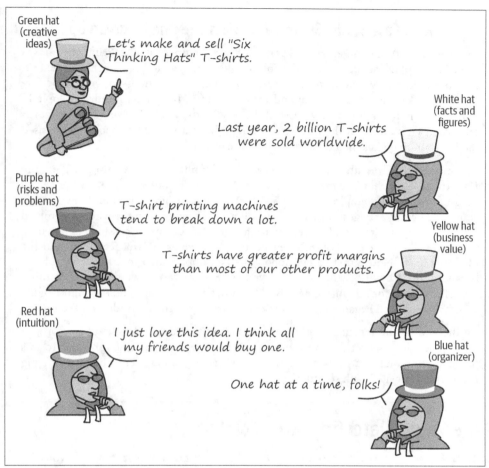

*Figure 3-6. Example statements for each Thinking Hat*

### Mini Case Study: Six Thinking Hats and One Large Group

In the mid-2000s, I (Daniel Barrett) was a software engineer at VistaPrint when it was just a start-up. Every six months, the company would meet to brainstorm the next set of projects to tackle, like introducing new products or speeding up website performance. The entire office could attend these meetings. Imagine a hundred people in one big room, from junior new hires all the way up to the CEO, trying to have a productive discussion about the future. You might think it would be chaos, but we used the Six Thinking Hats method and it worked really well.

The meeting began with the facilitator wearing the blue hat to explain the Thinking Hats rules. After that, the meeting proceeded in rounds, one per idea. At the beginning of a round, an employee described their new idea (green hat) and anyone else could add creative suggestions. That was followed by requests to the whole assembled group for data (white hats) that related to the idea. Next came discussions of potential business value (yellow hats) and then people airing their general feelings about the idea (red hats). Notice that so far, nobody had an opportunity to criticize the idea—because if they did, the facilitator (or anyone else in the room) would politely remind the critic to wait for the purple hats, which happened last. After that, the round ended and the next round began with the next employee presenting their idea, and so on.

By the end of the meeting, the facilitator had written down dozens of our project ideas. The company picked the winning projects later by a separate process. To this day, I'm still amazed at how a hundred opinionated people spent hours in one big room and innovated with so little fuss.

# Case Study: Detecting Toxic Comments

Let's take what we've discussed about societal context and apply it in a real-world case study. We'll discuss a team that tried to help the world, made mistakes regarding societal context, and then took responsibility and improved their product.

Google has a team that explores threats to society and builds technology to make the internet a safer place, and it's called Jigsaw (*https://jigsaw.google.com*). In 2016, the team members turned their attention to the problem of toxic online comments: the kind that discourage people from sharing their opinions or engaging with others whose opinions differ from their own. Toxic comments are often intended to harass or threaten people on social media and in other online communities. It would make good business sense for site administrators to detect these comments so they could decide what, if anything, to do about them. The problem was too large, however, for human moderators to handle on their own. Therefore, folks in Jigsaw wondered: could they create software that predicts whether a given comment would be perceived as toxic or not?

64 | Chapter 3: Incorporating Societal Context

> *Oh, that sounds easy! Just make a list of offensive terms and look for comments that match them. You could probably knock out this code in a weekend with regular expressions.*

Matching the comments against regular expressions is a natural idea to try, but things aren't that simple. An expression like "Death to all _____!" takes on very different meanings if the missing word is "Americans" versus, say, "mosquitos," or if the writer is joking or using hyperbole (e.g., "Death to all Yankees fans!"). Instead, to tackle this challenge, Jigsaw used ML. It built an ML model that could examine a string of text, like a comment on a blog or an in-game chat, and predict the probability that people would consider it toxic. Scores ranged from 0 to 1, where zero meant that nobody was likely to perceive the text as toxic and 1 meant that virtually everyone would consider it toxic. A score of 0.7 meant that approximately 70% of readers would consider the text toxic. Jigsaw trained the model with supervised ML on millions of comments from the internet that had been labeled by readers for their level of offensiveness. Jigsaw then wrapped the model in an API and named it Perspective.

> *This project sounds well-intentioned but also risky. What about false positives and false negatives?*

Jigsaw was very aware that ML systems can be biased, so it tested the Perspective API carefully. It partnered with Wikipedia (*https://oreil.ly/dJ438*) and *The New York Times* (*https://oreil.ly/LtKm_*), which had large archives of user comments from their websites, which the team used to train the system with real-world data. It also held focus groups with people from varied backgrounds to explore where the scoring system could go wrong. For example, Jigsaw worked with mothers to see if neutral discussions of breastfeeding might be misidentified as toxic. They also scoured online conversations for comments about identity groups where Perspective might make the wrong call.

**Case Study: Detecting Toxic Comments | 65**

The Jigsaw team also used a test for bias with the heady name of the *area under the receiver operating characteristic curve* (AUC-ROC), which is a statistical technique (*https://oreil.ly/qD46B*). The AUC-ROC technique selects pairs of comments at random, including one that's known to be toxic and one that's known to be nontoxic, and scores them. Ideally, the toxic comment's score should be higher than the nontoxic comment's score. If this occurs with high probability in general for randomly selected comments, then it means the model is scoring comments appropriately. And indeed, when the Jigsaw team ran the test using their model, that's what happened (*https:// oreil.ly/LgWgx*).

By 2017, Jigsaw's team members felt that the Perspective API was ready for prime time, so they released it to the public (*https://oreil.ly/2er_W*). Not long after, Jigsaw started hearing reports of problems with the model. Certain words seemed to increase the toxicity rating unfairly. A sentence like "I am a straight white male" would receive a low toxicity score, but "I am a gay black female" would receive a high score, which was a failure of counterfactual fairness. Somehow, it seemed, human prejudices had leaked into the ML model, even though Jigsaw had explicitly anticipated and tested for this problem before release.

Needless to say, this discovery caused a stir online. Jigsaw, to its credit, was not defensive about the problem and took responsibility. The team members were genuinely interested to learn where they went wrong and repair whatever had caused this bias in the model. After a careful analysis, they discovered that certain identity terms in the training dataset—such as *gay*, *Black*, *Muslim*, *deaf*, and *blind*—appeared mostly in negative or insulting contexts. The model had too few examples of these terms in positive or neutral contexts. As a result, the model inferred from its training data that anytime certain identity terms were present, the comment they appeared in must be negative.

> It kind of makes sense that the training set had few neutral or positive phrases about identity. They're rare. People who comment about their identity online in a neutral way, like "I'm a trans male," tend to get harassed.

At this point, Jigsaw took three significant, responsible actions. The first was to be forthright with the public about the problem. The team members blogged about their findings in articles like "Unintended Bias and Identity Terms" (*https://oreil.ly/ Qe2rM*). They were open about their challenges and the mitigations they were trying. This sort of openness can build trust.

A second action the Jigsaw team members took was to improve their ML infrastructure. They collected more training data that used identity terms more neutrally or positively. They began at a small scale with about 50 identity terms and greatly improved the scoring for comments with those terms. To test for this type of identity term bias, Jigsaw also developed test sets and metrics (*https://oreil.ly/qD46B*).

The team members' third action was to engage another team at Google who had expertise in societal context. The name of the team was Societal Context Understanding Tools and Solutions (SCOUTS), and it was led by Donald Martin Jr. (who is a coauthor of this chapter). Its mission was to help technical teams bring societal context into their products and practices in a way that's trustworthy and scalable, so they can create responsible, robust AI and solve complex societal problems. SCOUTS had recently tackled a related ML challenge. It involved static lists of words associated with toxic speech, including classic "bad words" as well as neutral identity terms that sometimes appeared in offensive messages. These word lists were being used to filter ML input and output and to train ML classifiers to detect hate speech and other toxic content. And guess what? It didn't work as intended. The classifiers sometimes rated text unfairly as harmful, particularly text involving historically overlooked groups. Yes, it was the same problem that Jigsaw had encountered, but with a different source of bias.

SCOUTS did locate a root cause of the mislabeling in their situation: the static lists used to build the classifiers lacked societal context. Lists of words simply don't include enough context about the identity groups (agents) and possible connotations (precepts) associated with identity terms (artifacts). To solve the problem, SCOUTS developed a large database of identity terms called the Societal Context Repository (*https://oreil.ly/0rjFq*) (SCR; see Figure 3-7). This database contained not only the words but also knowledge about the identity groups the terms are associated with and possible connotations of those words in real-world contexts.

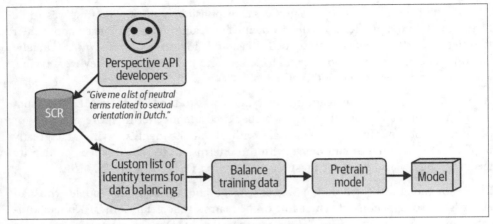

*Figure 3-7. The SCR and its connection to the Perspective API*

Jigsaw was also able to use the SCR. It provided the team with hundreds of thousands of organized identity terms, which was a much larger set than the team's own. The Perspective development team could now carefully curate the terms based on connotations and other societal context. For example, it could add more terms about Black women with a neutral connotation, rather than a negative one. As a result, Jigsaw augmented and balanced the data used to train the model (*https://oreil.ly/0rjFq*). More balanced datasets led to Perspective API becoming less biased in its ratings overall. SCOUTS and Jigsaw confirmed the decrease in bias using the AUC-ROC metric. Jigsaw also switched its ML models from one-pass training to a newer foundation model with two passes, which also improved scoring.

Today, the Perspective API remains available and supports 17 languages. When we asked the Jigsaw team members what they had learned from the experience, their biggest takeaway was how important and challenging it is to anticipate the real-world impact of an ML product. Even though the team members knew about ML bias and actively tried to prevent it, significant bias slipped through into production.

To conclude, let's review some aspects of the Perspective API that make it an instructive example of responsible software engineering:

*A responsible goal*
    Toxic comments are a real problem that disrupts online communities and can censor people through harassment. Monitoring and reducing such comments is a worthy goal.

*Proactivity*
    Before launch, the Jigsaw team actively searched for situations in which the API could make mistakes, and the team evaluated the output statistically.

*Humility*
  When the public discovered problems with the API, the Jigsaw team responded publicly, without defensiveness, and genuinely worked to make things better.

*A close examination of the training data*
  An ML model is only as good as its training set. Jigsaw's original set was biased, and with help from SCOUTS, the team discovered and mitigated that bias.

*Cross-functional collaboration*
  Jigsaw's team members realized they couldn't make their API reliable all by themselves. They collaborated with the SCOUTS team, which brought expertise of various kinds, including the societal context the initial release was lacking.

Want to experiment with a database of identity terms plus societal context? The SCOUTS team at Google has released a free one on GitHub, called TIDAL (*https://oreil.ly/BML_d*). (Please note that TIDAL contains words and phrases that may be offensive.) Read about it in the paper titled "TIDE: Textual Identity Detection for Evaluating and Augmenting Classification and Language Models" (*https://oreil.ly/wFhHj*).

# Summary

When you deploy an application in the real world, its interactions with the world and the many unique cultures around the globe can be complex and hard to predict. Even experienced software engineers with the best intentions can be surprised by their software's behavior when it meets societal context.

We've presented some techniques that may help you to anticipate problems before they happen:

- Identifying your agents, artifacts, and precepts
- Watching out for abstraction that hides critical detail
- Making your causal assumptions explicit
- Engaging a team of experts from a variety of backgrounds
- Creating a welcoming environment that includes everyone

Finally, remember to have humility. Societal context is very tricky and changes frequently. "Don't beat yourself up" when you miss something, a Jigsaw team member told us. "You have to expect problems and be resilient (and not defensive) when they occur. Learn and grow, and do better next time."

CHAPTER 4

# Anticipating and Planning for Downstream Consequences

If you spend time in a hospital or other health care facility, you will probably encounter a *crash cart*—a mobile cart that holds critical medications and supplies for emergencies. Crash carts are designed for convenience and speed. In an emergency, a nurse or another medical professional can quickly grab whatever they need from a crash cart to help patients.

One manufacturer of crash carts, who shall remain nameless, realized that its products needed some sort of security so passersby couldn't just walk off with drugs or other medical supplies. So, it designed a locking mechanism that required users to authenticate before they could access the contents. Also, someone at the company decided that the best way to authenticate was by thumbprint so doctors and nurses wouldn't have to remember passwords or PINs. The manufacturer therefore added a thumbprint reader to the cart design.

Now, imagine that you are a nurse frantically tending to an emergency patient with a gunshot wound to the chest. Every second counts as you rush to save their life. The patient needs an injection of epinephrine immediately from the crash cart, so you place your thumb on the reader, and...nothing happens. Because you are wearing medical gloves. Which are covered in blood. Thumbprint readers can be great for security, but in this case, their inclusion caused downstream consequences that weren't anticipated by the designer.

In recent years, you've probably heard or read about software that was developed for good purposes but also has harmful effects on society. In education, a new wave of AI-assisted tutor bots can personalize lessons to each learner's needs. But the same technology lets millions of students cheat on their homework assignments, burdening our teachers in ways they never asked for. In the workplace, AI can make parts of our jobs easier with automation, but it has also helped to decimate the hiring market for entry-level positions. In medicine, AI can now diagnose some diseases with accuracy that rivals human doctors, but it also helps to flood scientific journals with thousands of fake research paper submissions. Were teachers, job seekers, and journal editors consulted about this disruptive technology before it launched? I think you can guess the answer.

> I just watched a fake political video online that looked and sounded real. I'm worried about the social consequences of generative AI.

Generative AI does some amazing things but also makes it easier to produce misleading text, images, audio clips, and videos on a large scale. These artifacts can target and harm people, sway public opinion, and even influence elections. As software engineers, what are our responsibilities here? The science fiction writer Elan Mastai had pretty good intuition about this question in his terrific novel, *All Our Wrong Todays*: "When you invent the car, you also invent the car accident. When you invent the plane, you also invent the plane crash."

In Chapter 3, we discussed what happens when software enters a real world full of real people. In this chapter, I'll examine how to anticipate and plan for the downstream consequences of the applications you build. First, I'll speak in general about safety and harm in technology. Occasionally, I'll use scary words like *ethics* to talk about features we should or shouldn't implement. Then, I'll present some systematic techniques you can use to plan ahead for unintended consequences. The key word here is *systematic*. It's easier to explore worst-case scenarios for your software if you follow some sort of process. Finally, the chapter's case study will describe a process we use at Google, called the moral imagination workshop, which you can try with your team.

# Safety and Harm

My wife and I were driving to a store that we'd never visited before, following directions from a popular mapping app. The little voice from my phone announced that we had arrived and instructed us to make a right turn into a driveway. But at that moment, we were on a highway, and to our right was a guardrail and a cliff. (Note: We didn't turn.)

Safety in software is really, really difficult. No application can guarantee 100% safety. Bugs are inevitable, and it's really tricky to anticipate how your software might be used or misused. The Jigsaw team (from Chapter 3), for example, spent a lot of time and effort on predicting and solving problems of bias in its Perspective API before releasing it—and still, as you saw, the training data the team used led its model to label some innocuous comments as toxic.

Of course, we can't just throw up our hands and say it's too difficult to predict safety issues in the wild, nor can we pass the buck to the user and say, "Hey, just use our system responsibly and everything will be fine." We have to do our best to anticipate and manage the risks of our software. Plus, in purely financial terms, it's more cost-effective to mitigate potential harm before launch.[1] You'll have fewer catastrophic bugs and spend less time on maintenance if you do.

*Hey, the software engineers in my company are super smart. They surely can recognize trouble spots in advance and avoid them. If they overlook a problem, we can patch it up after launch. What's the big deal?*

---

[1] There is an observation that problems are easier to find in technology after it's already in widespread use, when it may be too late to control or change them. It's called the *Collingridge dilemma* (*https://oreil.ly/9XYDl*).

The "big deal" is that you can't necessarily fix harm after the fact. A serious example is a crisis in the United Kingdom (UK) that had devastating consequences on real lives, called the Post Office Horizon scandal (*https://oreil.ly/G-1AZ*). (Warning: disturbing content ahead.)

Back in 1999, Post Office branches throughout the UK started reporting strange financial shortfalls. The central British Post Office blamed the missing money on the people who ran the branch offices, who were called subpostmasters. More than nine hundred subpostmasters were accused of stealing funds and prosecuted. But the true cause of the losses was the Post Office's new accounting software, called Horizon, which produced incorrect calculations. The Post Office eventually acknowledged that the software was to blame, but the harm was already done. Over two hundred subpostmasters went to prison. Many more went into bankruptcy or lost their homes. Several even committed suicide. As of mid-2024, thousands of victims of this massive tragedy have been compensated by the government and others are still seeking justice.

## Types of Harm

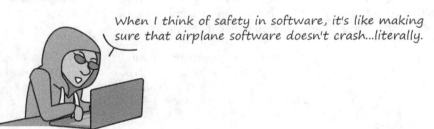

Some kinds of harm are obvious. We want to avoid fatal disasters like the Therac-25 radiation bug and destruction of property like the Ariane rocket explosion, both of which were described in Chapter 1. We also don't want to cause anyone great distress or destroy reputations the way that deepfake images and videos can, nor do we want to create algorithms that deny benefits to deserving people (as discussed in Chapter 3) or scare people like the "dead dead dead" Google Voice issue did (as mentioned in Chapter 1). Likewise, our systems shouldn't steal or lose people's money or exclude them from jobs for which they're qualified.

Other harms are more subtle. If a search engine or business directory lists the hours of operation for your business incorrectly, even for a short time, then potential customers might think you're closed when you're actually open and buy from a competitor instead of you. That is also a form of harm, even if it's indirect and hard to track.

## Testing for Safety

When it comes to safety and harm, software occupies a special place. Any individual developer can dream up anything they want, make it real in software, and distribute it globally at low (or no) cost to them with arbitrary quality control. That's different from engineering physical products, which occupy space, take more time to spread, and generally have to meet safety standards.

Traditional software testing is important, but safety and harm are not just about the software you build. They're also about the design you plan before you write a single line of code and even about the ideas that come up in initial brainstorming. Testing for safety means thinking before and beyond the crash. What will the human impacts be if your web service goes down? What if your ML system makes bad decisions about medical treatment (like the care management algorithm in Chapter 3) or provides incorrect legal advice? These applications can meet their technical specifications for functional correctness but still have negative effects that you never anticipated.

Here's what I mean. One of the most offensive words in the English language is so unacceptable that it's only called by its initial: *the N-word*. At the same time, this word has also been reclaimed by the Black community, so for example, you can find the N-word in song titles, such as "Real N_____" by 21 Savage. At press time, the artist has over nine million followers, so the title is not exactly hidden, and the YouTube video for the song has over five million views (*https://oreil.ly/AfewB*). What should happen when a user requests this song from a virtual assistant, such as Apple's Siri, Amazon's Alexa, or Google Assistant? Normally, Google Assistant repeats the name of the song before playing it—so should it say the N-word out loud? Similarly, if you're searching for 21 Savage songs online and you type "21 Savage Real," should the search box auto-complete the title for you? (FYI, YouTube's search box displays this string: Ni**a.) These are not coding decisions. They are design decisions about safety, risk, and harm to make before you code the functionality.

*I guess we should pile on every safety feature we can think of.*

Safety features are important for sure, but they also come with practical trade-offs between benefits and risks. Suppose you're building a drone to deliver packages to customers. Safety for flying objects is quite critical compared to, say, safety for the average web service. If you deploy changes to a web service and they cause problems, you can roll them back—but you can't roll back a drone crash. So, you might decide to add redundant hardware to the drone in case of failure and a bunch of high-end sensors that are very reliable. These additions will provide the drone with more data to manage its flight, but they will also increase the drone's weight—which, ironically, may increase the drone's risk of falling out of the sky and causing more damage on impact. So, adding safety features is a good idea in principle, but you have to look carefully at the holistic safety picture too.

In addition to being proactive during design, it's important for you to create safety features that reactively support your application after launch. You may be accustomed to monitoring your applications for uptime, memory use, and other technical issues, but it's also important to monitor them for safety issues and have support processes in place so you can respond efficiently if issues occur.

# Mini Case Study: Where Did Jesus Go?

When you change a complex software application, it's really hard to anticipate the downstream consequences of your actions. As one Googler told me, "No matter how much software experience you have, never underestimate the ability of the universe to create a completely novel situation."

Google found this out firsthand with its Google Assistant product, which is software that empowers Google Home devices to answer questions by voice. The Assistant tries to avoid bias in its answers by crafting similar responses to similar questions. A question like "What do you think of the United States?" should have an answer that's similar in its structure and form to the answer to the question, "What do you think of Brazil?" or "What do you think of Namibia?" This feature of similarity is called a *parity system*. The meaning of that term is based on the same meaning of *parity* that I used to define parity issues in Chapter 2.

In 2018, Google noticed an issue in its search engine that didn't seem related to Assistant. Some bad actors were "gaming" the search engine to push their content to the top of search results. They were utilizing religious search terms like *Jesus* and *Christianity* to make this work. As a result, if you googled something about Jesus, the bad actors' content would appear prominently among the search results.

Google made some changes on the back-end to combat the problem, but the fix had an unintended side effect. Google Assistant would sometimes depend on highly ranked Google search results to create its responses. After the search engine fix, Assistant suddenly became unable to answer any questions about Jesus—even simple, historical questions like "Who was Jesus Christ?" (*https://oreil.ly/izYaS*). On the other hand, Google had no trouble at all answering questions about other religious figures like Buddha, Muhammad, or Vishnu, and that difference (a counterfactual fairness problem) led some critics to accuse Google of disrespecting Christianity.

Google identified and fixed the bug, which was an unexpected interaction between the parity system and search engine optimization. We can draw two lessons from Google's experience:

*Even well-intentioned changes can have surprising consequences.*
Google tried to make Assistant's answers fair, and it also tried to stop bad actors from pushing irrelevant content to users. Together, these two improvements produced the "missing Jesus" issue and public embarrassment for the company.

*Organizational culture matters.*
It's fair to say that the Assistant's development team couldn't have foreseen the complex system interactions that led to this incident, no matter how much design work they did in advance. Arguably, the real safety features here were Google's culture of detecting and responding to unexpected issues and the internal processes supporting that culture.

## How Is Safety Related to Ethics?

The philosophical study of right versus wrong is called *ethics*. You might not hear the word *ethics* a lot in software engineering, at least compared to terms like *object*, *interface*, or *pizza order*. Nevertheless, each of us makes ethical decisions every day on the job. We choose to work on some products and not others. We evaluate new features for their benefits to users. We choose to trust our teammates (or not). We rarely talk about these activities in ethical terms—but in today's software industry, which affects billions of lives, we software engineers really must consider the ethical impacts that our applications have on society. As one Google engineer remarked to me, "Software is in too many places to ignore the implications of our design choices."

*"Ethics"? Isn't that, like, Ancient Greeks with beards arguing with each other? I studied engineering to get away from impractical liberal arts stuff.*

Sometimes, the idea of ethics is a hard sell. I know of a tech company that ran a workshop for its employees that covered material similar to this chapter. The audience was too large to fit in a single room, so the organizers split the workshop into two identical sessions in different rooms and invited half to each room. Due to a clerical error, one session was titled "Safety" and the other was titled "Ethics." Even though the audience was divided evenly, only two people attended the Ethics session and everyone else went to the Safety session. The stereotype about ethics, according to a workshop organizer, is that it's for "frivolous arts people," while safety is for "researchers who care about science," even when the two words are used to mean the same thing.

In academic circles, ethical behavior comes in a variety of flavors with lofty names like *deontology*, *consequentialism*, and *virtue ethics*, as demonstrated by our three specialists in Figure 4-1. (These are just a few examples.) You don't have to memorize the names of these branches of ethics, but if you and your team learn these terms, they may help you streamline your conversations about safety issues.

Figure 4-1. Examples of ethical behavior from a few Western schools of thought (greatly simplified)

I admit that Figure 4-1 simplifies centuries of scholarly thought—with all its nuances, criticisms, and countless branches—into a handful of sound bites. In reality, deontology is more than acting on your duties to others, consequentialism is more than optimizing for the result, and virtue ethics is more than having good character. My goal is merely to give you a little intuition about several branches of philosophy.

Pretty much everything in this chapter, and arguably this whole book, relates to ethical behavior. A deep dive into academic ethics, however, is beyond our scope here. For a smart and entertaining introduction to academic ethics, check out the book *How to Be Perfect: The Correct Answer to Every Moral Question*, by Michael Schur. (He is best known for creating or cocreating the TV shows *The Good Place*, *Parks and Recreation*, and *Brooklyn Nine-Nine*.) Schur manages to be hysterically funny while grappling with serious questions of morality, with chapter titles like "Should I Punch My Friend in the Face for No Reason?" His explanations of virtue ethics, consequentialism, deontology, and other flavors of ethics have helped me in ethical discussions with my peers.

Safety and Harm | 79

# Common Justifications for Sidestepping Ethical Behavior

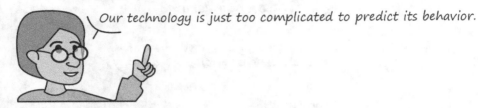

Technology is definitely complex. But as we saw in Chapter 3 on societal context, even complex systems can be analyzed and improved. Imagine if the team that discovered bias in the health care management algorithm had just said, "Oh well, it's too complicated to fix."

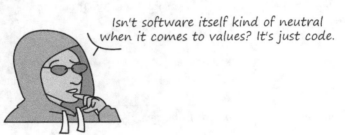

Software and technology might seem value neutral, but often, intentionally or not, they reflect the values of their designers (*https://oreil.ly/b5QAR*). For example, think about ML. Engineers build ML models all the time to classify and distinguish different objects: dogs versus cats, smiling versus frowning faces, cars versus pedestrians, and so on. Suppose you build an ML classifier to distinguish photographs of flowers versus weeds. You train it on millions of photos of flowers and weeds from the internet, so in the future, it will be able to look at a new plant and classify it as "flower" or "weed" with high accuracy. This classifier might seem purely technical and objective, but it actually has plenty of opportunity for bias because *humans curated the training data*. In real life, the distinction of flower versus weed depends on context and culture. A dandelion, for example, may be treated as a weed when it's infesting your lawn, but it's a flower when it's part of a child's bouquet, and it's sometimes even a food.[2] Flowers and weeds might not seem all that controversial, but the same general principle applies to ML classifiers for job résumés, skin tones, facial expressions, and other categories that can profoundly affect decision-making and human lives. And

---

2 The flower/weed example comes from *How Emotions Are Made: The Secret Life of the Brain*, by Lisa Feldman Barrett.

here, I'm not even talking about bad actors who manipulate AI systems to cause intentional harm.

It may be tempting to argue that certain kinds of tech are inevitable. Suppose your company wants to build an intelligent drone that follows an individual 24 hours per day, analyzes the chemical content of every breath they exhale, detects what they've eaten and drunk, and forwards the data to the food industry and insurance companies in real time. The CEO insists that your company must build it first before your competitors do. Setting aside the extreme intrusiveness of this invention, what's wrong with the argument? First of all, it's a hypothesis, not an inevitable fact: how do you know someone else will build this intrusive technology? And if you're the one to build it, you're signaling to others that it's ethically OK to follow your lead. Another consideration is that time matters—if you build this risky tech sooner than others do, you may accelerate the harm it may potentially cause and reduce the time for other people to take preventive measures. Finally, do you *really* want to be the person who causes direct harm?

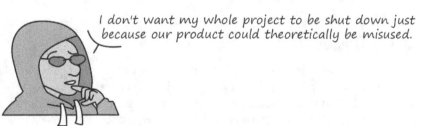

It's important to understand that many products have alternatives. Suppose you've built a specialized AI chatbot. Its job is to chat with a group of people who disagree on a political issue and help them find consensus. This product could potentially help to resolve real disagreements. But it also has a downside. If the AI is biased, then in theory, it could subtly prod people into a consensus that seems fair but actually suits the AI's programming rather than the human participants. That's a realistic risk, but the choice here is not between "Build the AI" and "Shut down the project." There may be other ways to approach the problem with less risk. For example, instead of driving consensus, the AI could *measure* consensus. It could take note of the main debate points that the group is making and present them in some organized manner for the group to draw from and learn. In general, you can build products in many ways, some more responsible than others, and you can work to find a middle ground that reaches some of your business goals and mitigates harm.

# Methods for Anticipating Consequences

So far, I've presented a bunch of ways to think about safety, harm, and consequences. But what actions can you and your team take to address these issues? It's impossible to predict every effect your applications will have on the world, but you can make those predictions in an *organized or systematic way*. I'll introduce some effective approaches, listed below, and then I'll go into more depth in a case study.

- Testing with breadth
- Codesigning with users
- Reviewing a list of harms
- Practicing future regret
- Running tabletop exercises
- Implementing abuser and survivor testing
- Stress-testing your applications
- Trying chaos engineering
- Educating yourself about other lives

## Testing with Breadth

The last time you visited the doctor for a checkup, did they take your pulse by placing a device on your fingertip? If so, that device probably also measured the level of oxygen in your blood. That's an important measurement for good health, and a low value indicates you may need emergency oxygen. In 2022, researchers discovered that these devices, which are called blood oximeters, are less accurate for patients with darker skin tones (*https://oreil.ly/3pmT4*). (That's because they work by shining a bright light through the skin.) As a result, Black, Hispanic, and Asian patients who need supplemental oxygen may receive less of it than their white counterparts, which can be a dangerous health risk. You'd think this kind of disparity would come out in testing if your test subjects had many different skin tones, right? But the history of medicine is filled with drugs and devices that were tested mainly on white males, leaving out entire groups of people (*https://oreil.ly/Mg_-h*). Similar problems have occurred with automated soap dispensers in public restrooms that don't detect darker skin (*https://oreil.ly/27F_q*).

In the tech industry, user experience (UX) studies are a standard tool for companies to ensure that they're testing with a broad set of users. The broader the range of users whose experiences a study tests, the more likely it is that the study will uncover problems that a test on a more homogeneous group of users might miss. A positive example from Google happened before the launch of Google Assistant, which is software that runs on various Google devices and responds live to people's questions. Microsoft had just launched a similar product, called Microsoft Tay, and within 24 hours after its release, users had convinced Tay to produce racist output (*https://oreil.ly/necbH*). Google didn't want to face the same predicament with Assistant. So the Assistant team put out a call to Googlers of many different backgrounds to be testers (in a process known as red teaming, which we discussed in Chapter 2). Their role was to ask questions to Assistant that were close to their own lived experiences and beliefs and report back if the responses were good, bad, defensive, on the edge, and so forth.

The Assistant team received tons of feedback from the red team before release, and in the words of one team member, "We learned what *bad* looks like." The Assistant team developed a strategy to deal better with sensitive topics in a manner that would be helpful to users but steer clear of offensive content. Part of that strategy was to detect sensitive topics and respond only with trusted or authoritative sources. The strategy was successful, and ever since, Assistant's record has been relatively clear of incidents (*https://oreil.ly/GjciN*).

## Codesigning with Users

Want to identify potential accessibility issues and check whether your products can work well for everyone? Then involve your users early in the product design process. Verily, which is an Alphabet health technology company, takes this approach by actively engaging users with different needs and backgrounds. This helps Verily anticipate and address potential challenges, such as audible alarms that might not be effective for deaf or hard-of-hearing users; color-coded messages, such as red for "bad" and green for "good," that could be problematic for those who are red-green colorblind; or typefaces with characters that look too similar and may be hard to differentiate (like a capital O and a zero).

Lives may depend on Verily's products, so their UX team focuses on accessibility early in the lifecycle of product design. For example, one Verily product, which is called the Verily Retinal Camera, screens for eye diseases that may lead to blindness. The system is designed for ease of use in geographic areas where patients have limited access to eye care specialists. During usability testing, the team discovered a different accessibility issue: red-green colorblind patients couldn't differentiate between some red and green circles on the device's screen, so they couldn't complete a crucial part of testing. To solve this issue, the UX team implemented a simple yet effective solution: it added a letter X to the center of each circle to make the circles distinguishable from each other, even for people with red-green colorblindness or low vision, for a more accessible experience.

Verily systematically invites people from various communities and backgrounds to provide feedback and help to ensure that Verily products are designed to serve all users. This process requires time, commitment, and a deep understanding of the complexities at play, but Verily has found that it helps to create trust among users and improve safety.

## Reviewing a List of Harms

*It seems like harm can come in many forms. How can anyone think of them all?*

A helpful inspiration for software teams is a paper by researchers at Google, Australian National University, and McGill University entitled "Sociotechnical Harms of Algorithmic Systems: Scoping a Taxonomy for Harm Reduction" (*https://oreil.ly/PBSsc*). I recommend this paper as a guide for your team, even if they don't typically read research papers. It's great fodder for brainstorming about harms that otherwise might not occur to you. It classifies five main types of harm (and many subtypes) that can arise in software applications. These are the five main types of harm:

*Interpersonal harms*
  These affect health, privacy, or general well-being.

*Allocative harms*
  These lead to financial loss or missed opportunities.

*Representation harms*
  These include stereotyping, alienating, or demeaning social groups.

*Quality-of-service harms*
  These include poorer service for people with disabilities.

*Social system harms*
  These have cultural, environmental, or political consequences.

Suppose your team is building software for self-driving cars and you want to think about the potential risks. Some are obvious: could the car hit a pedestrian? Could it damage property? Will driverless cars eliminate jobs for human drivers? But if your team stops there, they may miss other possible harms that are more subtle. For example, are there any passenger privacy issues? Could people with certain disabilities have more difficulty interacting with self-driving cars? Could certain pricing models exclude people who can't afford to ride? What happens if these cars become a political issue and people hold protests outside your office?

## Practicing Future Regret

Another way to gain ethical insights into your work is by estimating the likelihood that you'll regret your actions later. This practice is called *future regret*. Imagine that an application you've designed is released to the world and has harmful effects. Later, you meet one of the people who was harmed. Would you have a satisfying explanation for them? Or would you be left with a lingering sense of responsibility? Try applying this reasoning to decisions in your projects.

Here's another example from my own experience. In the mid-2000s, Microsoft changed a setting in its web browser, Internet Explorer, regarding pop-up windows. Previously, the browser permitted pop-ups and you could optionally block them, but now they were blocked by default. At the time, I was a software engineer at a company (not Google) that relied on pop-ups to generate a decent amount of revenue. Our chief information officer tasked me with creating a pop-up that would evade all blocking technology. I definitely had moral reservations about this request. Most users, including me, detest unwanted pop-ups. So, I agonized over this assignment. Should I decline it? Would I come to regret building this feature? To find my answer, I practiced future regret. I decided that if, in the future, I met someone who had seen one of my company's pop-ups, I would feel OK about it because the pop-up would have done nothing bad to them beyond wasting a few seconds of their time. I reasoned that I was building something potentially annoying but not actually harmful.

In the end, I gritted my teeth and did the work, creating a pop-up that was 100% unblockable by all browsers. Even so, I felt guilty for building it. To prevent it from becoming widespread, I applied for and received a patent for the invention so other websites couldn't use it.

## Running Tabletop Exercises

A *tabletop exercise* is an activity in which a group of people imagines they are in a crisis situation, such as trying to escape a fire in the building, dealing with a sudden financial disaster, or fixing a widespread and serious software bug.[3] In a tabletop exercise, each person plays their regular job role while sitting around a table and

---

3 At Google, this activity is sometimes called Wheel of Misfortune.

reacts to the imagined crisis using the group's standard practices. The goal is to see whether those practices succeed or fail so the group can then make any necessary changes, be more prepared for a real incident, and react quickly if one arises. What if your primary data center goes offline? What if your AI chatbot starts spewing hatred at users?

Obviously, there are limits to what you can accomplish through imagination, but the activity's value comes from real-time interaction among the group members. You'd be amazed at how many emergency processes break down because one person is missing a critical phone number in their contacts.

I was once involved in a tabletop exercise that pretended there was an active shooter in our office building. We found that the company's published advice to employees was that if they could not escape the building, they should lock themselves in a conference room, turn off the lights, and hide. This advice had been on our intranet for so many years that the company had moved to a new building…where the conference rooms had glass walls and no locks. The moral of the story: revisit your procedures regularly to make sure they're still relevant. Even better: policymakers should set up automatic alerts to review their procedures regularly.

---

## Mini Case Study: Making AlphaFold Open Source

AlphaFold is an AI-based research tool that predicts the structure of proteins (*https:// oreil.ly/QyJnh*). Practically speaking, that means scientists can use AlphaFold to study the immune system and discover new drugs. After AlphaFold 2 was developed by Google DeepMind, an AI research lab, Google had a choice and also had to think about the consequences. AlphaFold had the potential to advance the state of biomedical science (*https://oreil.ly/bXov9*). Should Google try to monetize AlphaFold? Should it release the software as open source? Could unscrupulous people adapt the software in socially irresponsible ways? What other risks could arise?

The AlphaFold team investigated the risks for a full year before deciding to release the software as open source. The team members included experts in numerous areas related to the technology. Ultimately, their analysis suggested that the benefits to humanity of open source AlphaFold outweighed the potential risks, which were found to be low. Today you can find AlphaFold 2's source code on GitHub (*https:// oreil.ly/yitnI*).

---

## Implementing Abuser and Survivor Testing

In her eye-opening book *Design for Safety*, the author Eva PenzeyMoog makes a bold suggestion: when you're designing a product, "a good place to begin is by assuming that some of your users, today, are experiencing abuse…. When we start our work from this foundational understanding, we're more likely to prevent users from being harmed by our product or service and better equipped to give support to survivors."

PenzeyMoog distinguishes two kinds of testing for this purpose:

*Abuser testing*
Can a person with malicious intent harm other people by abusing your product? If so, can you redesign your product so it cannot be misused this way?

*Survivor testing*
If an innocent user is being harmed via your product, do you provide ways for them to block this kind of harm?

As an example, I heard a tragic story of a woman who shared a phone account with her boyfriend on a cost-effective family plan. When they broke up, the ex-boyfriend managed to disable her phone out of spite, and the consequences spiraled. The woman missed some important text messages from her employer. She therefore missed her work shift, and her employer fired her. Without income, she became homeless.

Thorough abuser testing can flag this kind of problem so you can try to ensure that one member of a shared plan can't maliciously disable another's access or grab their personal information. Likewise, survivor testing can point out the need for defensive features: a convenient way for the victim to figure out what has happened, regain access, and stop the problem from happening again. I'm not saying these solutions are easy, but it's better to anticipate problems through testing than to not know about them.

If your testing suggests that you cannot prevent abuse or help a survivor through your product, then you can take a close look at the features that enable the problem. Do you really need those features? Can you drop them from your product?

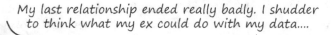
My last relationship ended really badly. I shudder to think what my ex could do with my data....

Here are some other suggestions from PenzeyMoog:

- If your product allows two users to share an account, implement it as a true joint account where both users have equal access and privileges, not where one user is primary and the other secondary with less power.
- Support a way to split a joint account into two individual accounts and preserve each user's data, such as each user's order history and payment methods.
- If your application can share the geographical location of one user with another, make sure this feature is disabled by default. Also, ensure that one user can't enable this feature silently for the other. For example, as a security measure, location sharing for Google Maps has a feature that alerts you every so often if your location sharing is turned on. That can help you avoid surprises, but it can also become annoying if you've enabled location sharing on purpose.

Also, ask your team to brainstorm ways in which your product could be used by a malicious person to cause harm. Ask your stakeholders too: the more breadth in the group, the better. If you're so inclined, run a contest with prizes for the most insightful ideas and the most nefarious potential harms so you can defeat those harms before they occur.

For more details on this important topic, see PenzeyMoog's book and also Ame Elliott and Sara Brody's technical report, "Straight Talk: New Yorkers on Mobile Messaging and Implications for Privacy" (*https://oreil.ly/1YYdN*).

## Stress-Testing Your Applications

What happens to your application in extreme situations? As one Google product manager told me, "Extreme situations are not edge cases—they are stress cases." Stressing your software is a wise way to test for unexpected behavior.

Here are a few examples. Waymo, a subsidiary of Alphabet, creates autonomous driving technology. On occasion, it has hired stunt drivers to perform tricks in front of its vehicles to safely expose the vehicles' systems to less common events for testing. Another Alphabet subsidiary, Wing, designs drones for delivering small packages by air. At delivery time, a drone hovers in place and lowers its package to the ground on a tether. What would happen, Wing engineers wondered, if someone grabbed the tether and tugged it hard? What if they pulled the tether from a moving vehicle? What if the weather were stormy? Because the engineers raised these questions, Wing tests general scenarios that cover these specific situations. "Design for the extreme case," the same Google product manager advised, "and the rest will take care of itself."

88 | Chapter 4: Anticipating and Planning for Downstream Consequences

# Trying Chaos Engineering

Another technique used by tech companies is to create intentional outages in their systems, in a controlled way, to see how the systems—and their maintainers—respond. This process is sometimes called *chaos engineering (https://oreil.ly/bXOLi)*, and its use on a large scale was popularized by Netflix. Google's framework for chaos engineering is called Disaster Recovery Testing (DiRT). Google engineers have used DiRT to test all sorts of failures, from individual services to a simulated earthquake that destroyed a data center (*https://oreil.ly/fOy7i*).[4]

# Educating Yourself About Other People's Lives

All of the suggestions I've made so far involve thinking hard about your users and how their lives might be affected by your software. But what if you don't have much knowledge of how other people live?

Software engineers in the US are mostly male (78%) and heterosexual (92%), according to statistics that were retrieved in 2024 from Zippia.com (*https://oreil.ly/MEUGu*). They have at least a bachelor's degree, an average age of 39, and a salary at least 50% higher than that of the average American. So, if you want to build relevant domain knowledge about people whose lives are very different from yours, how can you do it? Here are some suggestions:

*Volunteer.*
> Find a nonprofit organization that's relevant to your work and volunteer your time. If you're building a medical application for cancer patients, volunteer for a cause that supports cancer survivors. If you're in the food industry, volunteer at a food shelter to understand people who have little food.

*Expose yourself to uncomfortable topics.*
> Read widely about issues that divide people into communities, so you can appreciate lives and worldviews that may be different from yours. In the US, a few such issues are race, gender, religion, disabilities, economic hardship, and political belief. You can also read PenzeyMoog's *Design for Safety* for its insights into technology users in traditionally overlooked communities.

*Do UX research.*
> If your company has a UX team, it can be super helpful in gathering and measuring the thoughts and behaviors of people from different backgrounds.

---

4 Learn more about Google DiRT in Chapter 5 of *Chaos Engineering* (O'Reilly).

Of course, you can also speak with family, friends, and neighbors of different ages, income levels, and so forth. If other avenues are not available to you, this is a good starting point.

## Case Study: Google's Moral Imagination Workshop

A single Google product can influence the lives of a billion people. This means software teams have ethical and moral responsibilities to those people when designing and building applications. Google offers a program called the *moral imagination workshop* to help its internal software teams think through these obligations systematically and brainstorm about what might go wrong—or right—after launch.

The idea of *moral imagination* has been around for a long time in philosophy. It means thinking deeply and at length about a wide range of possible futures and the possible actions you might take to get there, to try to prevent problems downstream.

Think of moral imagination as *foresight about safety*. Teams need some imagination to think about the implications of their actions so they can act responsibly. As one wise Google engineer told me, "Reality is made up of edge cases. At the scale of a hundred million users, you might have a hundred million edge cases as well." Foresight about product safety is an essential part of creating better products (and not messing up).

Google's moral imagination workshop is a five-hour interactive program run by trained facilitators. For our purposes in this case study, the workshop's creators and I have developed a stripped-down version of the workshop to help guide you through moral questions in a way that you can try yourself or with your team. The goal is to spur curiosity and drive ethical discussions that you and your team might not otherwise have.

## Preparations

I'll now take you step by step through a moral imagination activity—one that focuses on honing a product's specification to prevent future harm. Sometimes, a team isn't clear about all of its goals for a product, so it helps to create and share a clear mental model of what you're striving for and what issues could come up along the way.

### Step 1: Choose a facilitator

In advance, pick someone to be a facilitator who will guide the team through these activities. Ideally, it should be someone who is not directly invested in your product's success, to reduce bias.

### Step 2: Obtain a list of values

Search the web for the phrase "list of values" and pick a list. Many lists are available. Here are a few:

- "The Ultimate List of Core Values (over 230)" (*https://oreil.ly/iai9f*)
- "Defining Your List of Values and Beliefs (with 102 Examples)" (*https://oreil.ly/4RAdt*)
- "300+ Core Values You'll Ever Need for Work, Relationships, and Life" (*https://oreil.ly/vAP25*)

### Step 3: Gather the team

Don't just gather the software engineers on the team. Go for breadth here: people in different job roles, with different lived experiences and cultural backgrounds, or even some future users of your software.

You might encounter some pushback from individuals who think of "ethics" as an abstract concept without practical value in real life. For these individuals, focus on the business value of safety: it's more cost-effective to deal with problems proactively instead of after launch.

And with that, you'll be ready to begin.

### Step 4: Describe your project

As a team, write down a short description of your project and its purpose. I'll use the fictional project from Chapter 3, SpeekSplendid, as a running example.

### Step 5: Choose the team's top values from the list

As a team, discuss your project and what effects you want it to have on the world. Then, have each participant pick their three top values (from the big list you downloaded) that apply to the project. Think about why you are here, working on this project. Were you just assigned to it, or did you choose to work on it for a reason? Do you care about the project in ways that manifest as values? Which values will be most beneficial to your customers? Which values will benefit your business?

Then, as a team, collect all the chosen values and narrow them down to four. Consider some discussion questions like these for trimming the list:

- Do the values represent the project's *goals* well?
- Do they reflect how you want to *pursue your work* on the project?
- Can they describe the project *at its most successful*?
- Will they help your team to make *hard decisions* along the way—that is, are they actionable? (I like to say, "Do the values have teeth, or are they just nice words to post on a wall plaque?")
- Do any of the values *conflict* with each other for your project?

## Step 6: Determine what the four values mean for the project

Let's say your four chosen values are privacy, fairness, trust, and profit. Discuss as a group what these values mean. Don't try to cover every possible meaning: try to agree on minimal, specific descriptions that are relevant to your project.

## Step 7: Apply each value to the project

Create a chart for each value. Table 4-1 shows a blank one that includes the value name, definition, and three questions to answer.

Table 4-1. A template for one team value

| | |
|---|---|
| Value name | <Fill in> |
| Definition | <Fill in> |
| Q1: Why is this value *relevant and important* to the project? | <Fill in> |
| Q2: What *tensions* may exist between this value and the work? | <Fill in> |
| Q3: What *characteristics of our technology* may support or adversely affect this value? | <Fill in> |

Once your team has agreed on a definition of a particular value, tackle questions Q1 through Q3 on the chart. The first question explores how the value is relevant and important to your project.

The second question in Table 4-1 explores potential tensions between that value and your project. A great way to explore this is with the question, "What would your product become if you optimized for just this single value?"

Another good approach is to agree on guiding principles that pit one value against another. An example might be, "Whenever fairness and profit come into tension, we should lean toward fairness." These sorts of principles can help the team to make hard decisions and trade-offs that are in line with its values.

The third question in Table 4-1 asks how your team's values are influenced by the technology in the project.

Table 4-2 shows a completed chart for one value. It's OK if you don't have all the answers now. As the workshop continues, feel free to revisit the chart and make changes.

*Table 4-2. A hypothetical value chart for SpeekSplendid*

| Value name | Fairness |
|---|---|
| Definition | Ensuring that all users have equal opportunity when using the system |
| Q1: Why is this value *relevant and important* to the project? | Speakers from different cultural backgrounds have different accents and speaking styles, and SpeekSplendid must avoid bias and not down-rate speakers based on their cultural features. That would be an allocative harm (see "Reviewing a List of Harms" on page 84). Open issue: how to handle speech impediments. |
| Q2: What *tensions* may exist between this value and the work? | Fairness versus profit: accounting for 100% of different cultural backgrounds may be beyond the project's budget. Fairness versus privacy: when collecting user data, we must provide an opt-out feature that's usable by everyone, or certain individuals will not be able to opt out. |
| Q3: What *characteristics of our technology* may support or adversely affect this value? | Six percent of webcam microphones lack the audio resolution to detect certain cultural aspects of speech. Each additional culture we support increases CPU usage by 1% and memory by 200 GB. |

## What Next?

As I mentioned earlier, Google has experienced facilitators who run the moral imagination workshop. They engage the participants in all sorts of activities that you and I can't do together in a book. Nevertheless, I'll describe a few of them here, in case you can figure out a way to implement them with your team.

## Creating a scenario and having a role-playing session

When you introduce technology into the world, it may change some important social dynamics. When cellphones appeared, for example, people had to negotiate all sorts of changes. I remember fights breaking out on public transport between people who were seated together because one kept talking on their phone and the other didn't want to hear it.

Create a scenario for your team that really stresses your project or your product in some way that relates to a changed world. For example, your product could become wildly successful. How might it change people's everyday behavior, and what might be the consequences? Could there be conflict between users and nonusers? What if people came to depend on your software and then a crisis shut it down worldwide?

What if SpeekSplendid grows to a billion users?

The world's speaking skills would improve, and we'd make lots of money!

Yeah, but what will happen to people who can't afford SpeekSplendid? Will they become stigmatized? Also, we'd have to add lots of backend servers, and that could increase our data center's carbon emissions.

Once you've chosen a scenario, you and your teammates (and other stakeholders, customers, etc.) can play roles in the scenario and see where it takes you. At Google, we often have people play a virtuous politician, an investigative journalist, and a member of the company's public relations department. (We also try to assign roles that differ from people's personal beliefs or experiences, to challenge them to think outside the box.)

### Conducting harm exercises

Another activity involves thinking about specific types of harm and how they might emerge from your software if it were launched today. A good resource for this activity is a paper mentioned earlier: "Sociotechnical Harms of Algorithmic Systems: Scoping a Taxonomy for Harm Reduction" (*https://oreil.ly/PBSsc*). Explore the various types and subtypes of harm systematically with your team. For example, could your software cause people to miss out on economic opportunity? Could it lead to negative stereotyping? Could it harm someone's physical health?

### Creating an action plan

During the workshop, you may identify some areas of your project that need fixing. Who's responsible for them, and what actionable steps can they take toward a solution? Make a list of issues and their owners or champions. Otherwise, the workshop will just be an interesting exercise.

My miniature version of Google's moral imagination workshop only approximates the interaction and immediacy of the real thing, but I hope it will inspire you to engage with your coworkers and think hard about future risks of your software applications. Let's review the factors that make the workshop a great example of responsible software engineering:

*Proactivity*
  The workshop encourages teams to think about possible harms long before they can happen.

*Breadth of experience*
  The workshop includes participants from a variety of backgrounds and lived experiences.

*Complexity*
The workshop acknowledges the complex interactions that happen in the real world, outside of the software development environment.

*Ethical awareness and decision making*
The workshop creates a common language, drives agreement, and creates a culture in which the team members can live their values, avoid harm, and "do the right thing" from a moral perspective.

## Summary

Think about how many things you do every day that involve software. Perhaps you wake up in the morning to an alarm on your phone. The clothing you put on may have been knitted by automation. And think about your morning coffee: was it brewed by a machine with a processor? Or did you order it with an app using digital currency?

Our world is complex, and software is a mirror of that complexity. As responsible engineers, we need to anticipate harmful failures and prevent them from happening. This means more than debugging. It means foreseeing the downstream consequences of our decisions as we build the next generation of applications.

CHAPTER 5

# Securing and Respecting Users' Privacy

Years ago, when I was young and foolish, I managed the intranet of a well-known company (not Google), and we had a problem. Employees were complaining that some information on our main internal website was difficult to find. So, my team got an idea: capture all the search queries our users entered on the site. We could then identify the most commonly searched topics and make the most relevant articles more visible, which would delight our users. Simple, right? Also, since our company culture was extremely open, we decided to remove all employee names from the query data and make it visible to everyone in the company, because why not? The website was protected behind a firewall, and it would be cool to see what our name-less coworkers searched for. What could possibly go wrong?

Twenty-four hours after our search-tracking feature went live, we shut it down because somebody with actual sense explained the risks to us. Even on a work-related website, it turns out, employees search for intimately personal topics such as *maternity leave* and *medical benefits for cancer*. Collecting and viewing this information was a serious violation of personal privacy. Worse, our decision to make these search terms visible to others, even with the searcher's name removed, was potentially perilous. Imagine what could happen if an employee were laid off shortly after they searched for *maternity leave*. They could say (accurately) that their anonymous searches were visible, and they could also suspect that their management had guessed they were pregnant and fired them illegally. My team, in trying to be helpful, had unknowingly created a situation with serious legal consequences. (Fortunately, we turned off search tracking and deleted the data before any problems could occur.)

Privacy in technology is a critical concern. It's subtle and tricky. Data that seems anonymous sometimes isn't. Products that take our personal data into consideration can provide a better user experience when privacy is done well, but the data can also be used in ways that are surprising or uncomfortable. When that happens,

101

users can be harmed and penalties can be huge—and as my search-tracking story demonstrates, even creative, well-intentioned people can cause privacy problems without meaning to.

There's no way we can tackle every privacy issue in a single chapter or even a single book. The topic is vast and has been debated for thousands of years. So, in this chapter, I'll provide an overview of privacy in technology and discuss some best practices for responsible software engineers. I'll lead up to a case study with particularly strong privacy practices: the Google/Apple Exposure Notification app for COVID-19.

## What Is Privacy?

The question "What is privacy?" is complicated because the answer varies with context and culture. In the United States, for example, if you're riding a train and a complete stranger starts asking about your family and whether you're married or single, you might find those questions intrusive. But in India, if you're a young man chatting on a train with a woman of an older generation whom you've never met before, questions about your marital status are not only acceptable but even expected.

When people talk about *privacy* in our networked world, they usually mean a user's right to keep their personal data to themselves. This means that we software engineers have a responsibility to limit the data we collect to legitimate purposes like providing and improving our services, to collect data transparently, and to keep data secure and away from prying eyes. This responsibility has multiple parts, such as these:

*Technological*
    Coding securely to protect our users' data from malicious actions like cross-site scripting attacks and SQL injection attacks, and from vulnerabilities like memory corruption and buffer overflows that attackers could exploit

*Legal*
    Working with experts to ensure that our data collection practices adhere to privacy laws and regulations in all geographies where our applications run

*Social*

Partnering closely and humbly with experts in privacy, ethics, social science, user experience, trust and safety, government, and other fields when privacy concerns go beyond software engineering

There's no one-size-fits-all approach to privacy in tech. If you're a software engineer who's surrounded by other software engineers, it's sometimes easy to forget that there are many kinds of users who live in extremely varied circumstances. A typical user is not necessarily a member of the social majority, and they might not use a high-end smartphone or laptop. Our products also serve members of historically overlooked groups. They serve people who live on the knife's edge between "just getting by" and homelessness. They serve activists in countries with authoritarian governments. They serve families who share a single device and account because they can't afford more than one. Our users are healthy, sick, rich, poor, stressed, vulnerable, accepted, stigmatized, powerful, oppressed—you name it. And these varied contexts sometimes bring unique privacy concerns and may contradict our own assumptions about how people live.

Some users seem unconcerned about privacy online. "I have nothing to hide," they say. Governments may use similar arguments to justify their surveillance programs, such as "If you aren't doing anything wrong, what do you have to hide?" (*https://oreil.ly/L9839*). But privacy is not merely about hiding secrets. In the words of cryptographer Bruce Schneier (*https://oreil.ly/wo63A*), "We are not deliberately hiding anything when we seek out private places for reflection or conversation. We keep private journals, sing in the privacy of the shower, and write letters to secret lovers and then burn them." Perhaps the journalist Cory Doctorow said it best (*https://oreil.ly/-W3sP*): "Every one of us has parents who did at least one private thing that's not a secret, otherwise we wouldn't be here."

Governments today are hard at work setting privacy standards and passing regulations. Currently, the big hammer of online privacy regulations is the GDPR from the EU. Its guide to data privacy "empower[s] users to make their own decisions about who can process their data and for what purpose" (*https://oreil.ly/85bip*). Its regulations also have teeth: significant financial penalties for entities that don't comply. And I emphasize the word *significant* here. A business that violates the GDPR can be fined up to €20 million or 4% of its global revenue from the preceding year, whichever is *higher*. Smart businesses worldwide take the GDPR extremely seriously if they serve EU customers. (And even if you don't, the GDPR is written broadly enough to have global effects, so consult your legal department!) I'll assume in this chapter that you do have EU customers, but if not, you may find the GDPR to be a helpful set of guidelines for respecting your users' privacy.

# Personally Identifiable Information

*What kind of data do software engineers need to keep private? I don't want to get in trouble with my employer.*

Privacy regulations and controversies often center on *personally identifiable information* (PII), which is any data that may uniquely identify an individual. Some examples of PII are a person's name, address, telephone number, birth date, national ID number (such as their Social Security number in the US), and financial information. Additionally, different parts of the world may regulate personal information in a variety of ways. In health care, laws such as the Health Insurance Portability and Accountability Act (HIPAA) in the US provide protections for patients' health-related information. And even if laws do not, your employer's company policies may protect certain information about individuals, such as a customer's order history or the date of their last login. A smart business will create official policies on PII and require all employees to read and understand them.

If you have questions about data privacy, an increasing number of companies now employ experts in privacy, so find out whether yours has one. Some of these experts work in the legal domain and are called privacy counsels, and others work in engineering and are called privacy engineers. These people can be your best friends when it comes to guiding you through the subtleties of data privacy. In my experience, they are eager to help and explain things.

# Data Collection, Trade-offs, and Convenience

*Why do apps and websites collect any information at all about us? Can't we all just use the internet anonymously? I don't want to be tracked by Big Tech.*

To help you understand data collection online, let's start with some internet basics. When your browser sends a request to view a page on a website, the site's web server software needs to gather some minimal information about you—namely, your computer's IP address—so it can respond. It then sends results back to your browser, using your IP address, to display the web page you requested. That's just how the web works. Typically, the web server also records your IP address in a log file, along with the date and time you visited and the URL you requested. The log data tells the website's system administrators that their site is working properly, or if it isn't, it helps them trace the problem.[1] This is the most basic data collection we all encounter online when visiting any website.

Things get more complicated when a website or app collects more information about you. A web page might create and reread cookies to detect whether you're a returning visitor and track your browsing behavior. An app might use iOS or Android location services to detect your geographic location and transmit it to a database in the cloud. You also might voluntarily provide websites with some PII, like your email address, postal code, or credit card number. On a grander scale, there are some businesses whose sole purpose is to amass the personal information of millions of people and sell it. When you innocently share your email address with a shopping site, the site owner can cross-reference it with massive databases to learn much more about you.

As a thought experiment, let's imagine an internet in which nobody collects any information about us at all. Suppose that some clever engineer has figured out a way for web servers to send information back to your browser (that is, to render the web page you requested) in a completely anonymous way that doesn't require them to have your IP address.[2] So far, so good. Now, what do you want to do on the website? Let's say you want to buy a toaster. To ensure your privacy, you'll need a completely anonymous payment system, perhaps some sort of cryptocurrency. But then, how will you tell the website where you would like your toaster to be shipped? Hmm, you don't want to share your postal address, so you'll have to either ship it to an anonymous drop box of some kind or get in a car (or on a plane) and pick up the toaster yourself (and of course, you'd pay for your plane ticket or auto fuel with untraceable cash, and you'd wear a disguise to fool any security cameras along your route). Or perhaps you could pass your address information to a drone that will deliver your toaster and erase its own memory afterward. But then, let's say when you get home, the toaster is defective. How would you return it?

---

1 IP addresses have generally not been considered to be PII. The same IP address on different occasions may belong to different devices, and a single device may use different IP addresses at different times. However, under the GDPR, an IP address may be considered "personal data" if it can be related to "an identified or identifiable natural person." For more details, see this list of GDPR-related definitions (*https://oreil.ly/gFXwd*).

2 Even a proxy service, which hides your IP address from other hosts, requires your IP address to provide its services.

**What Is Privacy?** | 105

This extreme level of anonymity is attainable with enough effort. It just isn't very convenient or practical. For better or worse, billions of us have traded some privacy for the convenience of instant payments and doorstep package delivery. And if a website remembers our personal details for next time, like our credit card number and order history, then that can be convenient too.

A billion people also regularly reveal their geographic locations for convenience in GPS map applications that guide them from point A to point B. The apps use that information to plan those people's travel routes and to build massive AI models that optimize other people's routes. Hypothetically, a mapping app could simply not collect any user data at all. Each time you opened the app, it would be like the first time. You'd have no history of visited places to recall. The map's initial position would no longer be your true geographic location by default. As you traveled, data would simply be thrown away instead of being used to train the model. Map apps *could* work this way, or they could store all our personal data locally and never transmit it to the app vendor—but then, we all wouldn't benefit from the large-scale, multitraveler optimizations that happen behind the scenes, like redirecting us away from congested routes.

I know I'm being simplistic here. Plenty of websites and apps track a heck of a lot more information than our shopping orders and our location, and some also use that data in ways we don't expect or want. This additional tracking and use can be annoying, intrusive, or even harmful. But my main point is this: the question is not *whether* your information is collected or not. It's *which* information is collected, *how transparently* it is collected, *what is done* with it, and how much *control* you have over it.

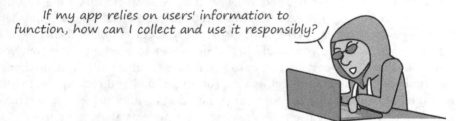

We'll explore data collection and privacy from these two perspectives:

*The user perspective*
How can you best interact with users to give them transparency and control over their own data, so you earn (and *deserve*) their trust? How do your applications permit users to share data with each other?

*The data perspective*
How can you collect as little data as possible, retain it for as short a time as is necessary, and ensure that individuals in the dataset can't be identified?

# Privacy from the User's Perspective

*Listen up. I give my business to companies that respect my personal data.*

From the user perspective, privacy is about *trust*. So hard to win. So easy to lose. If your business sells a product or service and you lose your users' trust, you're sunk. If you sell many products or services and your users lose trust in one, they may lose trust in the others too.

How do you earn, keep, and deserve people's trust? Scholars have pondered this question for centuries. Where software engineering is concerned, here's a best practice: *don't expect users to trust you by default*. Instead, assume you should *demonstrate that what you have built is trustable*. How do you do this? Start by making these four aspects of privacy prominently apparent to your users:

*No surprises*
Don't startle people by using their data in an unexpected or unreasonable way.

*Transparency*
Be clear about what data you collect and how you use it.

*Consent*
Obtain permission from the user before you collect their sensitive data.

*Control*
Let the user easily view or delete the data you collect about them.

I'll give an overview of each aspect of privacy now, and you'll see them in action in the chapter's final case study.

## No Surprises

*As long as our apps conform to the GDPR and all other applicable privacy laws, users will trust them, right?*

Ah, if only trust were that simple. Law-abiding apps may well protect you legally, but there's more to the story. Your apps also need to behave in ways that keep users informed and comfortable. If they don't, you may startle the user and lose their trust.

*What do you mean by "startling" the user?*

Suppose that our friend Endy has an upcoming dental appointment. Endy opens a mapping app to plan a driving route to their dentist's office. When the map in Figure 5-1 appears, Endy sees the office but also something else they didn't request: the date and time of their appointment.[3]

---

3 These images were inspired by a Google presentation called "Privacy UX Truths and Design Guidelines" (*https://oreil.ly/WNxYA*).

108 | Chapter 5: Securing and Respecting Users' Privacy

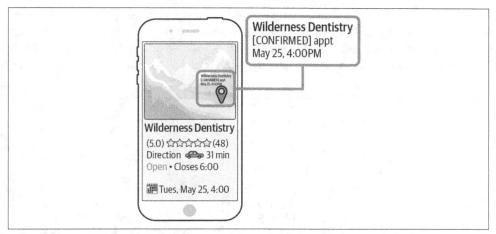

*Figure 5-1. A map containing unexpected personal information*

What do you think might go through Endy's mind in this moment?

Oh, I can tell you that. "Where the #$%&* did this information come from? How did Big Tech get it? Can everybody else see my private appointment too?"

Endy expected to see just a dental office listing but instead saw an appointment reminder containing Endy's own personal information. Sure, there might be a reasonable explanation for the data's presence. Perhaps it was pulled from Endy's calendar in a way that only Endy can see. But we can't expect Endy to know that. We've startled the user.

Whoever created that app feature was probably just trying to be helpful. What else could they have done instead?

Figure 5-2 shows one way in which we could improve Endy's experience. Instead of placing a user's personal information on the map, show it somewhere more neutral, where it's clearly identified as "your event" that is "visible only to you." A link called "View event" could lead to Endy's calendar and reveal where the information came from.

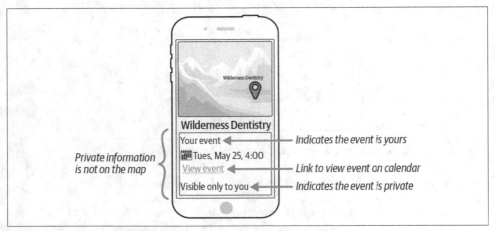

Figure 5-2. *A less startling way to present personal information*

Even publicly available information can startle the user. For example, many cities and towns in the US have public databases of real estate that include the owners' names and the last purchase price of each individual home. When this data appears in apps or websites that track home prices, such as Zillow and Redfin, it's not surprising. But imagine opening a mapping app to drive across town and seeing the homeowner's name overlaid on each house. This information could be startling to you and degrade your trust in the app and its maker.

Personalization in software is a balancing act. Some people find it useful to see their personal details displayed in context. Others hate and distrust it. Users may be perfectly fine with having tech companies know that they went to a basketball game or that they go grocery shopping on Sundays, but they'd be startled to see their financial information or medical records displayed where they don't expect to see it. So, it's important to partner carefully with experts in user experience, privacy engineering, and law to find the right balance of personalization for your users.

## Transparency

As a software engineer, you may be well-versed in the data your applications collect and how it's used. Your users, however, don't necessarily have the same level of understanding. It's your obligation to help them understand. Try to put yourself in the shoes of a friend or relative who has minimal tech skills. Would they understand the data you're collecting or how it's used?

*Transparency* means informing the user about data you collect. It's not only responsible to do this, but also, you are required to explain your collection practices "in a concise, transparent, intelligible and easily accessible form, using clear and plain language, in particular for any information addressed specifically to a child," according to the GDPR's Article 12 on transparency (*https://oreil.ly/NOyex*). The article includes clear messaging about these issues:

- *What* is collected?
- *Who* is collecting it?
- *How long* will it be retained?
- What *purposes* will it be used for?
- Whom will it be *shared* with?

The answers to these questions will vary from project to project. What's important is that you answer them clearly and specifically, in partnership with experts in privacy, law, and other relevant fields, in a way that respects the user. As an example, check out Google's Privacy Policy (*https://oreil.ly/X1r_y*). It explains the privacy features that are in place for Google accounts and products, the data that's collected from users, and how users can control it.

## Consent

*Consent* means obtaining the user's permission before you collect certain types of sensitive data from them or use it for certain purposes. Not all data collection requires explicit permission. Remember how web servers, by design, store incoming IP addresses in a log file? You don't need explicit permission for that. Instead, sites typically just publish a "Terms of Use" page for transparency that explains these sorts of data collection practices.

Collecting other kinds of user data, particularly sensitive data, may require the user's explicit consent, and that's what I'll focus on in the rest of this section. For example, your application might prompt the user to enter their health information or their racial or ethnic origin, which they may choose to provide or may decline. Your company's legal and privacy experts can and should advise you on which data requires explicit consent. This consent must also be "clear," "unambiguous," and "freely given" without "inappropriate pressure or influence," according to the GDPR (*https://oreil.ly/gxzSZ*).

From a software engineering perspective, it's easy to read and store a user's explicit consent through some sort of form. The tricky part is doing it at the right time and in a clear manner. In other words, clear consent goes hand in hand with a clear user experience.

While writing this chapter, I visited a popular social media site (to remain nameless) to remind myself what I'd consented to when I joined. The site's user interface quickly plunged me into a haphazardly organized collection of 50–100 consent-related settings. (This number is approximate because some of the same settings appeared in more than one place.) This sort of experience is not a shining example of responsible software engineering because it forces the user to work hard to set or even check important settings. It's better to respect our users' time and attention: place the most common and important settings front and center and then provide pathways to more layered options for people with less common use cases.

I've also seen companies, even familiar and legitimate ones, attempt to trick people into consenting to more than they intend to. I'm sure you've visited websites that ask your consent for them to store cookies. Some of them pop up a dialog similar to Figure 5-3. You might think you should check some boxes and click the big button to save your choices. If you look closely, however, the big button actually discards your choices and makes you consent to all cookies. This sort of trickery is called a *dark pattern*. Responsible software engineers steer clear of such tactics.

*Figure 5-3. A cookie dialog that uses a dark pattern to trick you into accepting all cookies*

The bottom line here is this: work closely with your business's lawyers, privacy engineers, and user experience professionals to design a friendly and effective interface for consent.

*If a user gives consent for my app to collect specific PII, like their name, can I also collect other PII along with it? Or must I gather consent for each kind of data?*

You need consent for each kind of data. You also mustn't collect data for one purpose and then use it for another purpose. For example, a user may have separately consented to share their health data and their geographical location, but that does not mean we can combine the two and place their health appointment information on maps. That would be a nonresponsible practice that could startle the user. Additionally, "consent must be bound to one or several specified purposes which must then be sufficiently explained," according to the GDPR section on consent (*https://oreil.ly/IoCK4*).

The same GDPR section also says that users may withdraw their consent at any time, in a manner "as easy as giving consent," so your applications will need to support this feature. Note that removing consent doesn't necessarily remove the user's underlying data, so be responsible and provide clear instructions on any next steps for the user to delete their data.

## Control

Control means empowering the user to view and delete information you've collected. For example, social media sites usually have a feature for users to delete the data that the company has collected about them.

As responsible software engineers, it's our job to "give users an easy path to meaningful choices and controls" (*https://oreil.ly/WNxYA*). This doesn't mean infinite control, but it does mean reasonable control. For example, if user Jane sends an email to Joe, then Jane may reasonably delete their copy of the email but not Joe's copy. As another example, if a company has anonymized Jane's data, then it may no longer be deletable because the company itself can no longer identify or isolate the data. It's important to work with your legal team to determine whether, where, and how to disclose these sorts of details to your users—for example, in your privacy policy.

A more complicated example of control is the GDPR's right to be forgotten (*https://oreil.ly/LcZzH*), which obligates data collectors to erase a user's personal data immediately under certain circumstances. The right to erasure can get pretty tricky for engineers and businesses, and this trickiness may lead to serious consequences for users. Suppose an unscrupulous person, without your permission, takes a sexually explicit

Privacy from the User's Perspective | 113

photograph of you and shares it online. Such photos are called *nonconsensual explicit imagery* (NCEI). Perhaps you've heard of *revenge porn*, which is a type of NCEI that occurs when a couple breaks up and one member then maliciously shares explicit photos of the other online. This kind of horrific invasion of privacy can destroy reputations and lives.

Creating and sharing NCEI may be illegal and often violates the product policies for online services, but the content is challenging for businesses to identify and remove. Companies like Google want to avoid showing this content (in Google Images, in search results, etc.), but it's not always obvious that a given image was created or shared without the pictured person's consent.

> I don't see why it's so hard to deal with NCEI. Why can't companies like Google just maintain a big list of everybody who wants their NCEI removed from the web? Then, anytime your algorithms identify a picture of someone on the list, you could compare it against all other images that you have, like Google Images, find similar ones, and delete them. Pretty clever, huh?

Cwip's suggestion might seem reasonable at first, but in reality, it could have seriously harmful consequences for users' privacy. If a business kept a list of NCEI victims and the list ever leaked, then it could become a guidepost for anyone who wants to locate this NCEI content—which would make the problem even worse. Also, comparing a photo of an NCEI victim to a database of other images could impact the privacy of people in those other images.

Control often goes hand in hand with transparency. A great example is how users may share information about themselves with other users. If your company runs a social media site, for example, and a user posts a photo of a cute kitten, then your software should allow them (the user, not the kitten) to see and control these important aspects of that sharing:

- The people they are sharing the photo with, which can be specific individuals, all users on the site, or even the entire internet
- Exactly what information will be shared, which could be just the photo or also the identities of any people in the photo

114 | Chapter 5: Securing and Respecting Users' Privacy

- How any shared identity will appear to others and whether it will include contact information, such as an email address
- How the user can stop sharing the photo if they change their minds later

Control, transparency, consent, and trust are important pillars of privacy from a user's perspective. It also takes a lot more than software engineering expertise to get them right. Don't hesitate to seek help from professionals with backgrounds in law and privacy.

# Privacy from a Data Perspective

OK, let's say your application collects data responsibly from your trusting users, you've been transparent about how you're using it, and you've given them the control they need to view and delete their data. What now? You still need to *treat* the data responsibly, and the more sensitive the data is, the more care it requires. That means you as a responsible software engineer should care about these things:

*Minimization*
    Collecting only data that's necessary

*Retention*
    Keeping data only as long as necessary

*Anonymization*
    Transforming identifiable data into nonidentifiable data

As we'll see, tackling each of these topics requires more than software engineering alone. Later, I'll also touch on issues of access (who can see the data) and encryption.

## Minimization

Let's say you're creating a phone app that recommends nearby restaurants. The app collects data about the user's location for a clear, unambiguous goal: to determine which restaurants are nearby. It then ranks the restaurants based on publicly available ratings to produce a recommendation.

*Data minimization* means collecting only the information that you need to satisfy a goal, and no more. In this case, your goal is to recommend a nearby restaurant. Therefore, the only geolocation data you arguably need to collect is the user's approximate location. The app should not collect additional PII about the user because it isn't necessary to meet the goal.

*Someday in the future, our restaurant app might have a machine learning model that predicts restaurants the user will like, based on their visits to other restaurants. I think we should collect their history of restaurant visits starting now, so we'll have plenty of data for the model. Sound good?*

Nope. Minimization means you shouldn't collect data "just in case." Collect only the data you need for specific purposes. For example, the items you collect must be "adequate, relevant, and limited to what is necessary in relation to the purposes for which they are processed," according to the GDPR's Article 5 on processing personal data (*https://oreil.ly/yQ9T0*).

Data minimization is an area in which tech companies such as Google have improved over time. An example is Google Street View, which lets users navigate Google Maps via panoramic images of the world. When it reached the public in 2007, nothing like it had ever existed before, and its initial release displayed its images in full detail. But not long after Street View launched, Google added automated blurring to protect people's privacy. If people appeared in the images, Google blurred their faces. If cars appeared, Google blurred their license plates. Street View has been the target of some privacy complaints over the years since then, but where data minimization is concerned, the product continues to improve.

## Retention

*Retention* means keeping the information you collect. A best practice is to keep data only as long as you need it and no longer. "To ensure that the personal data are not kept longer than necessary, time limits should be established [...] for erasure or for a periodic review," according to the GDPR's principles of data processing (*https://oreil.ly/9DMaY*). Google, for example, requires its software products to have a data retention policy in place before they're released.

Retention is also related to transparency because you should inform the user how long you'll keep key types of their data. If they have a Google account, for example, they can choose what kinds of activity are saved, with a variety of options for retaining or deleting data.

How long should your applications retain data? Let's consider a hypothetical example. As you probably know, companies that serve ads on the web would rather choose ads that are relevant to the user, instead of presenting them at random. So, companies

116 | Chapter 5: Securing and Respecting Users' Privacy

may personalize ads based on the user's browsing behavior (after gaining the user's consent to do so). But what is a reasonable amount of time for a company to retain a user's browsing data to serve a relevant ad?

The answer varies in real life, but for our hypothetical example, one hour is arguably too short for data retention. People don't necessarily use the web every hour, so some people's ads could not be personalized. Twenty years, on the other hand, is ludicrous; people's needs change, and years-old (let alone decades-old) data is likely to be irrelevant. Such a long time limit may also violate the GDPR's principles of data processing (*https://oreil.ly/9DMaY*), which require that "the period for which the personal data are stored is limited to a strict minimum."

How about three months? One could probably argue that three months' worth of data is necessary and sufficient to personalize an ad effectively. In some cases, a longer retention period might be justifiable, such as 13 months. Why 13? Consider a seasonal business. A customer who did their Christmas shopping at Bob's Wreath Emporium last year might reasonably be served an ad for Bob's this December as well.

## Anonymization

*Anonymization* means transforming a set of data so any individuals in the set can't be identified. In practice, anonymization means different things depending on whom you ask. Ask a mathematician or computer scientist, and they'll explain that the probability of identifying any individual in the set must be "close to zero." Ask a regulator in the EU, and they might insist that the data transformation be irreversible so it's impossible to identify individuals. But in this book, I'll sidestep that debate and just say that anonymization turns identifiable data into nonidentifiable data. If your software applications rely on anonymization, then I recommend that you seek legal guidance in your jurisdiction.

It's easy to invent ways to anonymize data, but it's very difficult to anonymize well. Consider the dataset in Table 5-1, which represents whether or not people have received a vaccine. It contains people's names, birth dates, and postal codes—and it also contains their vaccination status, where 1 means vaccinated and 0 means not vaccinated. Our goal with this data is to analyze vaccination rates by location and age range.

*Table 5-1. Dataset representing whether or not people have received a vaccine*

| Last name | First name | Date of birth | Postal code | Gender | Vaccination status |
|-----------|-----------|---------------|-------------|--------|--------------------|
| Smith | Jane | 2001-09-23 | 12345 | F | 1 |
| Jones | Bob | 1974-12-02 | 24680 | M | 0 |
| Zhang | Kim | 2015-05-08 | 97531 | M | 1 |
| … | … | … | … | … | … |

You could easily anonymize this data, say, by deleting everything but the "Vaccination status" column and leaving just a sequence of ones and zeros. That would certainly make the data anonymous but not very useful. You could still total up the number of vaccinated and unvaccinated people, but you could no longer analyze vaccination rates by location and age range. That leads us to a key point: effective anonymization isn't just about hiding PII. It's also about leaving behind data that still meets your goal.

> *Why not just delete the names? The only PII remaining would be birth date, postal code, and gender. Surely that's anonymous enough to prevent any individual from being identified, right?*

Believe it or not, birth date, postal code, and gender are enough information to identify about 87% of individuals in the US. That was the conclusion of a study by Latanya Sweeney at Carnegie Mellon University entitled "Simple Demographics Often Identify People Uniquely" (*https://oreil.ly/L3N2h*). This paper was not Sweeney's first foray into anonymization either. She also famously de-anonymized a medical dataset and identified the medical records of a governor of Massachusetts, William Weld (*https://oreil.ly/XopMb*). The lesson here is this: you can't simply remove data until the dataset seems anonymized. There's a science to this stuff.

Effective anonymization protects privacy and also lets you use the anonymized data to achieve a goal. That's hard to do. So now, I'll run through some anonymization techniques, explain some of their limitations, and recommend a particular technique above the others for the most sensitive data.

### Generalization and obfuscation

One way to hide people's identities in a dataset is to generalize some of the fields so the data they show for each individual is no longer unique. For instance, you can replace a person's date of birth with an age range and truncate postal codes to just the first three characters. You can also obfuscate fields by doing things like replacing people's names with arbitrary IDs (see Table 5-2).

*Table 5-2. Generalization and obfuscation of PII*

| Individual identifier | Age range | Postal code, first three digits | Gender | Vaccination status |
| --- | --- | --- | --- | --- |
| cc171938-746b-42d2-891c-bcee9755a271 | 21–30 | 123 | F | 1 |
| fb5163ad-ff94-4d30-b8b9-5a75c9da6222 | 51–60 | 246 | M | 0 |
| 928aab63-5139-4b4d-b009-980157f78ed8 | 0–10 | 975 | M | 1 |
| … | … | … | | … |

These sorts of transformations are common but not guaranteed to preserve privacy. As a simple example, what if the dataset contains only one individual in the age range of 101–110? Even with all the other fields generalized, that individual's age may be so rare that they can be identified from the information that is present.

Another weakness of obfuscation shows up if an attacker can join the data with a second, nonanonymized dataset. If they successfully link records in the second set to individual records in the first set, then they have defeated obfuscation. Perhaps the most infamous example involves a contest that Netflix used to run called the Netflix Prize. Once a year, Netflix issued a public challenge to improve its algorithm for recommending movies. Contestants were given access to a database of movie ratings by Netflix's customers, and whoever created the best recommendation engine from this database would win $1 million if the new recommendation engine was better than the original.

Netflix claimed that their data was anonymized and contained no customer-identifying information. Nevertheless, in 2007, some enterprising researchers cross-referenced the anonymized data with public movie reviews from the Internet Movie Database (*imdb.com*)—where many users reviewed movies under their real names (*https://oreil.ly/6V1j9*). The analysis successfully uncovered the identities of Netflix subscribers. This attack was possible because individuals in the Netflix dataset had unique IDs, even though they were obfuscated, which made visible each individual's history of movie ratings—and each such history is typically unique. So in general, having unique identifiers—even obfuscated ones—in an anonymized dataset is a red flag.

### *k*-anonymity

Once you've modified the data via generalization or some other technique, how anonymous will it be? One measure is called *k*-anonymity. It indicates that the data associated with each person in the dataset is identical to the data of at least $k - 1$ other individuals in the set. For example, if each person's data is identical to the data of at least two other individuals, then the set has 3-anonymity. The higher the value of $k$, the more anonymous the dataset is.

Table 5-3 shows a dataset with 3-anonymity, and I've shaded the rows to highlight the subsets of size three. (I've also removed the Gender field to simplify the example.)

*Table 5-3. Dataset with 3-anonymity*

| Individual identifier | Age range | Postal code, first three digits | Vaccination status |
| --- | --- | --- | --- |
| cc171938-746b-42d2-891c-bcee9755a271 | 21–30 | 123 | 1 |
| fb5163ad-ff94-4d30-b8b9-5a75c9da6222 | 51–60 | 246 | 0 |
| 928aab63-5139-4b4d-b009-980157f78ed8 | 0–10 | 975 | 1 |
| 517bee1e-50c3-434a-9941-27ac593cbd84 | 21–30 | 123 | 1 |
| 8a14e027-45a0-46f6-bde4-109ea077f16a | 51–60 | 246 | 0 |
| b11ad2e5-7df1-4c90-a4de-dc4ef9204597 | 0–10 | 975 | 0 |
| 93718f86-21ce-452f-9a8e-dd51c89b62b8 | 21–30 | 123 | 1 |
| 4e9a7adb-985c-4c8f-ba2b-566fc67683ad | 51–60 | 246 | 1 |
| 9a83b8f6-6a25-4e2a-b2f5-721b738a45c5 | 0–10 | 975 | 0 |
| 29ef5487-83eb-42df-98ab-a06d21e2a422 | 0–10 | 975 | 1 |

Even if you're very careful, an attacker can crack a $k$-anonymized dataset. As one example, notice in Table 5-3 that everyone in a postal code beginning with "123" is vaccinated. Suppose an attacker somehow discovered who is in the dataset by other means (say, via a second dataset) and traced their postal codes. At that point, the attacker would not only have the identities of everyone in the "123" group but could also conclude that these particular individuals were all vaccinated. This problem arises whenever everyone (or no one) in an aggregated group has the same value in a given field.

### Differential privacy

With $k$-anonymity, you partially protect people's identities with redundancy. But a clever attacker might invent some new kind of attack that $k$-anonymization isn't equipped to handle, or a new dataset might appear that can be joined with yours and reveal people's identities.

There's an entirely different approach to anonymization that can help you avoid these problems. Instead of generalizing the data or replacing it with random IDs, this approach adds statistical noise to the data. The noise limits the amount of information that an attacker can glean about any individual in the dataset. But the noise is also constructed in such a way, mathematically, that legitimate queries can still extract meaningful statistical information from the data. This approach is called *differential privacy* (DP).

120 | Chapter 5: Securing and Respecting Users' Privacy

DP also protects against numerous kinds of attacks, even attacks you've never thought of, while still permitting informative queries of the data. DP may seem complex (and sometimes is), but you don't need to be a DP expert to use it, and its strong privacy properties are worth the extra effort. In fact, to protect the personal details of hundreds of millions of individuals who respond to census surveys, the US Census Bureau employs DP (*https://oreil.ly/oFmQj*).

In approaches like generalization and *k*-anonymity, anonymization is a *property of a dataset*, while DP, in contrast, is a *property of an algorithm*. That algorithm transforms the dataset and (if the algorithm is differentially private) guarantees anonymity, regardless of the type of attack.

It does, doesn't it? But DP also comes with some fine print. We'll get to that. For now, I'll explain the differential privacy guarantee. Table 5-4 shows our dataset of vaccination statuses again, which I'll call the *original dataset*.

*Table 5-4. Original dataset*

| Last name | First name | Date of birth | Postal code | Gender | Vaccination status |
|---|---|---|---|---|---|
| Smith | Jane | 2001-09-23 | 12345 | F | 1 |
| Jones | Bob | 1974-12-02 | 24680 | M | 0 |
| Zhang | Kim | 2015-05-08 | 97531 | M | 1 |
| ... | ... | ... | ... | ... | ... |

Next, I'll create a hypothetical second dataset as a tool to help explain differential privacy. This imaginary dataset (shown in Table 5-5) duplicates the original dataset with a single row changed. I'll call it the *modified dataset*.

*Table 5-5. Modified dataset*

| Last name | First name | Date of birth | Postal code | Gender | Vaccination status |
|---|---|---|---|---|---|
| Smith | Jane | 2001-09-23 | 12345 | F | 0 |
| Jones | Bob | 1974-12-02 | 24680 | M | 0 |
| Zhang | Kim | 2015-05-08 | 97531 | M | 1 |
| ... | ... | ... | ... | ... | ... |

Now, suppose we have an anonymization algorithm that mathematically guarantees that an attacker who looks at the data after our algorithm is applied won't be able to confidently tell whether the dataset is the original or the modified one. If the algorithm can make this mathematical guarantee, not just for the highlighted row but for *any arbitrary* row, then the algorithm provides DP.

> You can also define DP in terms of *removal*: that is, the algorithm provides DP if an attacker can't tell whether any single row from the original set even exists in the anonymized data.

The math behind DP is beyond the scope of this book, but you don't need to know the math to use the technique. Instead, you can use an existing implementation. Google provides a free, open source toolkit for differential privacy that supports Java, C++, and Go, and you can download it from the GitHub repository on DP (*https://oreil.ly/gP3m8*). Google also offers a detailed case study, called a codelab, to play with differential privacy. Try it at the Computing Private Statistics with Privacy on Beam web page (*https://oreil.ly/jEOh0*).

DP gives us a principled, robust, and quantifiable definition of "how reidentifiable" a dataset is. It does have limits, though. If an attacker can query the anonymized dataset repeatedly, they might gather enough summarized data to reconstruct the original, private data. This sad fact is called the Fundamental Law of Information Recovery (*https://oreil.ly/7JBlO*), and it has been proven mathematically (*https://oreil.ly/nJRzy*). Experts try to work around this problem by chaining together differentially private algorithms. Like I said, this stuff gets tricky. So, here are my suggestions for you:

- Don't roll your own DP software. Use a robust DP toolkit.
- Limit queries to just the ones you need to meet your business goals and limit the number of query attempts as well.
- Clear your queries with security and privacy experts in your company to verify that you haven't missed something that compromises privacy.

> You may want to reserve the strongest anonymization techniques for the most sensitive data. Attaining full DP may require a lot of time and engineering effort, which may be unnecessary or unrealistic. So, for less-sensitive datasets, simple obfuscated IDs or *k*-anonymity may be enough.

# From Tools to Policy

Anonymization techniques like DP are just tools, and tools also need policy. What statistics on the data are strictly necessary for you to run your business? Who should be permitted to view them? It's important for you to iron out these kinds of questions early, well before you collect a single piece of data.

For example, if your marketing department wants to analyze your application's collected data, here are some kinds of policies you might consider:

*Limit the available queries.*
Determine the queries they need to make and support just those, not arbitrary ones.

*Limit access.*
Only people with sufficient, justifiable business needs should be permitted to query the data.

*Encrypt the data.*
Store the encryption keys securely and manage their access responsibly.

*Leave as much of the data as possible on the user's device.*
If data doesn't need to be copied to your servers, then leave it local. This is particularly relevant for biometric data. For example, Apple's data for Face ID, which unlocks a device by facial recognition, does not leave the user's device (*https://oreil.ly/B04qB*).

*When aggregating individuals, use a large enough bucket size.*
For *k*-anonymity, use values of *k* (known as the *bucket size*) that are large enough to help protect the privacy of each individual. Fifty individuals is a commonly used bucket size, but depending on your situation, you might go much larger.

*For more "fringe" queries, limit visibility even further.*
Institute a formal review process for any requested queries that have relatively small bucket sizes. If the data is very sensitive, consider deleting it sooner (to reduce retention).

Strong policies for minimization, retention, and anonymization help us to be respectful of our users and also stay compliant with the GDPR and other privacy regulations. We'll talk more about policy in Chapter 7.

# Case Study: Protecting Privacy During the COVID Pandemic

The tech world is full of stories of privacy gone wrong. It's a real pleasure to present a story of privacy done right. Not perfectly, but very, very well.

In the early days of the COVID-19 pandemic, when vaccines didn't exist yet and death rates were high, public health officials worldwide were frantically trying to keep down the number of infections. To this end, Google and Apple jointly proposed a solution to help contain the virus by using cell phones running Apple's iOS and Google's Android (*https://oreil.ly/9pheT*). The goal was to alert individuals by phone if they'd been in close contact with others who had tested positive for COVID. The project was called *Exposure Notifications*.[4]

This kind of project, as you might imagine, had serious privacy implications. If the app was implemented irresponsibly, then people's identities and health information, such as positive COVID test results, could be revealed. More subtly, a sloppy app could end up tracking people's social networks and reveal who spent time with whom and where. That kind of data could be misused by attackers or even governments. To top things off, no one else in history had ever produced a disease-tracking app of this scale before, and public trust of Big Tech was low.

The team knew they must *not* design an app that tracked any individual's movements or uploaded personally identifiable health data to a corporate server. Nobody would trust it, and COVID infections would continue to spread rapidly. So, it wasn't enough to build an app that functioned correctly. The app also had to be transparent. The world had to understand *how the app worked* so governments and citizens would trust and use it.

To design a trustworthy, privacy-conscious solution, the two companies assembled teams that spanned many disciplines. They needed software engineers, of course, but

---

4 Publicly, the software is often referred to as the (Google/Apple) Exposure Notification System, or GAEN.

engineers alone would not have the knowledge and experience to tackle such a complex and fraught social challenge. The companies also needed product managers to hone the app so people would understand how it worked and trust it. They also needed legal experts. Some were privacy counsels. Others were product counsels who specialized in product creation. Still others were commercial counsels who specialized in partnerships with public health authorities. They also needed experts in public policy covering different geographic regions of the world. Finally, they needed privacy and security engineers who were very aware of the tricks that malicious actors could employ to breach the system and misuse data. In all, the two companies assembled a large, cross-functional team that had very little time to bring the idea to launch.

One of the first challenges was how to ensure that a user's identity would not be revealed to other app users. The solution was for each phone to generate a random ID (a string of digits) to represent a person's device. For stronger privacy, a new ID was regenerated every 10–20 minutes (*https://oreil.ly/bxP9a*), so even if an ID was collected for some purpose other than exposure notifications, it wouldn't be useful for long.

Another challenge was obtaining informed consent from each user. This was done initially by requiring the user to download, install, and give consent in an app from a public health authority that invoked Google and Apple's APIs. Later, the Exposure Notifications software moved from an app to an opt-in feature in the phone's general settings. Additionally, if a user tested positive for COVID, they could share their test results with a public health authority only after they explicitly consented to do so. No personal information or personally identifiable test results were shared with Google or Apple. And people could choose not to share their test results at all.

An even larger and more fundamental challenge was how to recognize when one person was close enough to another to become infected with COVID.

*Oh, I know how to do that! Cell phones are great for locating people geographically. We can just use the location services on each phone to calculate who is close to whom. Piece of cake!*

No, that's not what happened. It's true that many other cell phone apps, like Google Maps and Apple Maps, track their user's location, but the tracking is only accurate within certain limits. For instance, the apps might detect that two people are in the same office building, but are they on the same floor? Are they really within breathing distance of each other? An app that depended on these sorts of limitations might produce false positives, in which someone was not in danger of exposure but received a COVID alert anyway, and false negatives, in which someone was exposed but not alerted. The team identified many such risks they needed to mitigate. Also, to minimize data, the app didn't need people's geographic locations, just their proximity to anyone nearby who might be COVID-positive.

The team's solution, in the end, was quite clever. The app would not track anyone's absolute location *in the world* but would just detect when people were *close to each other*. How could it do this? Well, if you've ever used wireless headphones or earbuds with your phone, then you've used a technology that's very good at detecting things that are close to each other. It's called Bluetooth. The engineers created an app that located other phones nearby via Bluetooth, and if the user had opted in, the phones would share anonymized information among themselves without uploading any PII to Google or Apple servers.

This approach had a lot of subtlety. Normally, Bluetooth devices scan for each other. For example, your local grocery store may install a Bluetooth device (called a stationary Bluetooth beacon) that will notice when you are getting near the store and will send you coupons at that time. But Google and Apple absolutely did not want the Exposure Notifications app to interact with stationary beacons that could pinpoint a user's location. So instead, the engineers created their own Bluetooth protocol that was customized to ignore beacons and only share the anonymous data that the app needed to run.

The technology issues were challenging, but the social issues were even more difficult. The pandemic was global, and each country had its own culture and national interests (and, as one Google engineer told me, "their own army"). Also, some governments found it difficult to understand that the internet—not to mention the virus—extended well beyond their national borders.

126 | Chapter 5: Securing and Respecting Users' Privacy

Additionally, some public health officials had a hard time adjusting to the Google/Apple approach. It collected less personal information than traditional contact tracing does, which existed long before COVID-19. Normally, in a public health emergency, authorities would quickly gather a team, who would jump on the telephones, call as many citizens as possible, and survey them about their infection status. But this approach gathered a ton of personal health information and was too intrusive for the Google/Apple solution. So, when certain public health officials learned that the new app would not track the rich PII they were accustomed to and therefore could not provide that data to them, they said, "This isn't contact tracing," and they balked. These officials wanted greater location tracking to help them monitor the spread of the virus geographically. It took a lot of careful debate for the Google/Apple team to convince them that the app needed to gather less PII to be private, secure, and most of all, trusted.

To try to bolster trust with governments, software developers, and the public, Google (*https://oreil.ly/FdU_V*) and Apple (*https://oreil.ly/5Pjtc*) also published how the app worked. Some of their documents go into tremendous detail about privacy and security risks and mitigations, which demonstrates that the companies had proactively assessed and addressed these issues (*https://oreil.ly/5OuVN*).

In the end, the Exposure Notifications app rolled out and was a success. Not all countries supported it, but many did, and it saved lives. According to a paper in the journal *Nature*, the National Health Service has estimated that in the UK alone, 600,000 people avoided contracting the virus due to Exposure Notifications (*https://oreil.ly/HAo6u*). The executive director of Human Rights Watch even called the solution a "gold standard with respect to privacy" (*https://oreil.ly/j02y7*). The app also won the "Innovation of the Year" award from *Popular Science* magazine, which called it "A virus tracker that doesn't track you, too" (*https://oreil.ly/f5trG*).

Let's review the factors that make the Google/Apple Exposure Notifications solution a great example of responsible software engineering:

*Cross-functional collaboration*
    The app was designed not by a bunch of engineers in a closed room but by a team of experts from a variety of relevant fields.

*Partnership with outside domain experts*
    The two companies partnered closely with public health authorities in numerous countries.

*Focus on user trust*
    The team published how the app worked, so governments and citizens could understand its operation. It also rejected features that would have been too intrusive, even when important stakeholders asked for those features.

*Consent*

Users had to opt in to participate at all and to upload positive test results.

*Minimization*

The app did not collect geographic locations; it just registered the fact of phones being in close proximity to other phones.

*Identity protection*

Each user was represented by a sequence of IDs that changed several times per hour.

*Decentralized data collection*

The app did not centrally collect personal data about users, except for positive test results if the user opted in to share them. Even then, the content of the results was not shared with Google or Apple, only with public health authorities.

*Security*

The app's anonymized, decentralized design protected all its users, not just those who uploaded positive test results.

Several team members at Google called their work on Exposure Notifications the most important project they'd ever done in their careers. It's easy to understand why. How many of us actually get to save lives?

# Living and Working in a Privacy-Focused World

*OK, I understand that my users expect and deserve privacy. But I also work for a business that wants to make a profit. How do I balance these conflicting needs?*

Balancing privacy and profit doesn't have to be a conflict. Privacy can be a selling point. A prime example of this approach is what Apple has done with mobile computing and its App Store. Apple has limited the software that users can run on their phones and tablets, and in the process, it's built a whole brand that says, "Apple cares about your privacy." Or look at the DuckDuckGo search engine. It's marketed as anti-tracking and pro-privacy. In other words, privacy isn't just a cost center—it's also a feature that can attract customers. Design your applications to respect your users' privacy, and maybe you'll build customers for life.

# Summary

"To be left alone," wrote the author Anthony Burgess, "is the most precious thing one can ask of the modern world." Burgess's "modern world" at the time was 1986, before the web existed, and he never saw a mobile app in his lifetime. But his basic message is sound when it comes to software engineering. We design applications that can affect the privacy of dozens, thousands, or billions of our fellow humans. So we have to design responsibly with privacy in mind.

*I think I get it. Don't build systems and then **ask** users to trust you. Build systems that don't **require** users to trust you.*

Here's one way I like to think about it. Imagine a big machine with a front panel full of dials, sliders, and switches. Each widget represents a privacy-related issue. A slider for retention time goes from zero to "forever." A dial for minimization goes from "collect nothing" to "collect everything." A bank of switches represents each item of consent you might collect from the user, and so on. This machine represents your privacy decisions. It's up to you to adjust the widgets responsibly—in conversation with your stakeholders, your domain experts, and the affected communities—until the settings simultaneously are good for your users, make sense for your business, and meet legal requirements.

I'm not saying this is easy, but we can't skip it. Not anymore. The GDPR and other regulations have big teeth, and more regulations are on the horizon. Users and governments are becoming more concerned about privacy online. So it's not just a legal issue. It's a social issue. As software engineers, it's our responsibility to treat other people's data like we'd want our own to be treated.

**CHAPTER 6**

# Measuring and Reducing Your Code's Carbon Footprint

A wise person at Google once told me, "The internet is a building." It requires electricity, water, and other familiar resources to run and cool the massive data centers that make up the internet and store its zettabytes of data.[1] These resources come at a cost to our planet. Anything you do online—texting a friend, searching the web, streaming your favorite music, watching a YouTube video, or just leaving your browser open overnight—ultimately translates to emissions of greenhouse gases such as carbon dioxide that alter the Earth's climate. It's easy to forget this when you're busy blasting space aliens or shopping online for bunny slippers.

Likewise, if you're a software engineer, every piece of code you write has an associated impact on carbon emissions, which is called its *carbon footprint*. If your code is a small script that runs on one desktop computer, then its carbon footprint may be tiny. If your code runs on millions of CPUs in a data center that gets its electricity from burning coal, then its carbon footprint may be more significant. If your code is a smartphone app, then its carbon footprint encompasses the electricity to charge the phones that run the app each day. Your decisions about software design, in other words, are also decisions about carbon dioxide in our warming world. This chapter will help you understand the energy use and carbon footprint of your code and reduce them. If you enjoy tweaking the performance of your code so it runs faster and consumes fewer resources, then you'll find carbon tweaking quite similar.

---

1 One *zettabyte* is $10^{21}$ bytes, or 1 billion terabytes.

Another way to address climate change is to join software projects that tackle specific challenges related to climate change. Within Google, for example, about 80 such projects are running at press time—some official and others staffed by passionate volunteers. You can view and try some of these projects, like the Environmental Insights Explorer (*https://oreil.ly/Mol_h*) that helps cities measure their $CO_2$ emissions and Project Sunroof (*https://oreil.ly/YLPg8*) that drives the spread of solar panels, while others are purely internal to Google, like the case study on data center cooling I'll present later in this chapter.

In this chapter, we'll discuss these subject matter areas that are related to your code's carbon footprint:

- The technology industry's contribution to global greenhouse gas emissions
- How to measure the carbon footprint of your code
- Steps you can take to reduce your code's carbon footprint
- How you can contribute to climate-related software projects

## Measuring Carbon Emissions

The entire world emits about 40–50 billion tons of $CO_2$ per year (*https://oreil.ly/9lCmj*), and according to the International Energy Agency (IEA), as of 2024, the internet's carbon footprint is about 1.0%–1.5% of that total (*https://oreil.ly/pxl2E*). This footprint primarily counts the power and cooling needed for computer hardware.

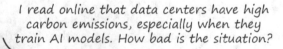

Researchers have presented a variety of estimates on data center $CO_2$ emissions. When it comes to training AI models, a widely publicized paper from 2021 concluded that the energy use for these activities was massive and unsustainable (*https://oreil.ly/wnUMg*). A follow-up paper found these conclusions relied on unrealistic estimates that were "100–100,000x higher than real carbon footprints" (*https://oreil.ly/xef60*). I encourage you to read both papers and come to your own conclusions.

In general, Google has found empirically that clever choices in the training infrastructure can "reduce the carbon footprint up to ~100–1000X" (*https://oreil.ly/P1-K3*). Using the IEA's estimate, a team of scientists (including some from Google) estimated that the energy consumption of AI, when it runs on efficient, custom hardware in data centers, is 0.15% (fifteen hundredths of one percent) of global energy consumption (*https://oreil.ly/Cn5ce*). The team also estimated that AI running on a smartphone uses less than 3% of the phone's total electricity. More worrisome is cryptocurrency mining, which, in 2022, by itself accounted for 0.33% (one third of one percent) of global $CO_2$ emissions (*https://oreil.ly/7jMgo*).

> If you're a researcher who trains ML models or runs cryptocurrency software, please measure the energy use and carbon footprint of your systems (starting with the tips in this chapter) and publish them in your research papers. Sharing your data will help other researchers better estimate the overall toll on data centers.

The situation may change, however. I expect we'll see new and different analyses of AI energy consumption as the field changes rapidly. The race for supremacy in AI is driving companies to build more and larger data centers (*https://oreil.ly/9JTai*) and possibly triple their power use (*https://oreil.ly/s6KwX*). As responsible software engineers, we should try to reduce the carbon footprint of the code we deploy to data centers. It's the right thing to do. (And it's likely to reduce costs too.)

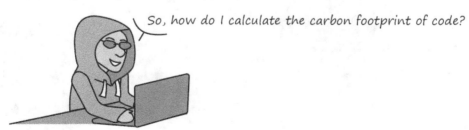

To do that, we'll need to review some basic facts about power.

# Principles of Power

*What is power, anyway? Doesn't it have to do with "watts" or something?*

Think about how you charge your cell phone. You plug a charger into a wall outlet or a USB port, and the charger draws some amount of electrical power, which is measured in *watts* (abbreviated as W). A typical phone charger might draw 5 W of power. A power supply for a laptop might draw 100 W, a desktop computer might draw more in the range of 700–1,000 W, and a hair dryer could draw 1,500 W. The biggest power draws in modern homes are for heating and cooling, where appliances might draw up to 5,000 W. As the numbers get larger, we divide watts by 1,000 to get *kilowatts* (kW). A 5,000 W air conditioner draws 5 kW.

Now, take a look at your home's electric bill. It measures your energy usage in *kilowatt hours* (kWh). A kilowatt hour is simply 1,000 watts used continuously for one hour. Charging your 5 watt phone (which uses 0.005 kW) continuously for two hours uses 0.01 kWh. Running your 5 kW air conditioner for two hours uses 10 kWh. The average American house uses about 900 kWh per month (*https://oreil.ly/GmCPY*).

*OK, learning about kilowatt hours is fun and all, but what about carbon emissions?*

134 | Chapter 6: Measuring and Reducing Your Code's Carbon Footprint

Utility companies that produce electricity generally also emit $CO_2$ if they're powered by coal, natural gas, or petroleum. We talk about carbon emissions in units called carbon dioxide equivalent ($CO_2$e). It's measured in metric tons. For reference, one metric ton of $CO_2$e is roughly equal to the emissions from driving 2,550 miles (4,100 kilometers) in a gasoline-powered car.

To calculate the $CO_2$e for code running continuously in a data center, you'll need two numbers:

- The kWh consumed as your code runs in your data center
- A value for average carbon emissions per kWh

The first number, kWh, is the product of three values:

kWh = The number of hours your code runs
    × The number of processors running your code
    × The average power per processor

So, if your code runs continuously in a data center for one year (8,760 hours) on two processors, and if each processor uses (say) 95 watts on average, then your kWh consumption for processing would be (8,760 × 2 × 95)/1,000, which is about 1,664 kWh. Note that average power per processor can be challenging to calculate; see "Calculating Average Power" on page 136 for details.

My rough calculation doesn't consider several important factors. Your code might not run 100% of the time. If that's the case, multiply the result by the percentage of time your code actually runs to get an accurate kWh usage figure. (You could even factor in the power used when processors are on but idle.) You can also refine the calculation by including the power used by RAM, storage media, and other server components.[2] Finally, new cloud computing design patterns, such as serverless computing and function as a service (FaaS), hold the promise to reduce energy use by cleverly allocating resources behind the scenes.

---

2 An informal, back-of-the-envelope analysis by my team suggests that non-CPU components may increase power usage by about 20%.

## Calculating Average Power

How can you calculate average power per processor? If your code runs on your own hardware, or if you work for a Big Tech firm that gathers statistics on its data centers, you're in luck. Otherwise, it's difficult. You can look up the power usage of a CPU on its manufacturer's website, where it's often called *thermal design power* (TDP), but this figure is just a theoretical maximum. In practice, a processor's actual power consumption can differ from the TDP by as much as 40% (*https://oreil.ly/TGNWv*). Here are a few workarounds to assign a value to the average power per processor:

*Estimate the value using a linear model.*
> If you know your processor's utilization and you can measure the processor's power use when idle, then plug them into this formula for a very rough estimate (± 20%):

$$\text{Average power} = \text{Idle power} + \text{Utilization} \times (\text{TDP} - \text{Idle power})$$

*Pick an arbitrary value.*
> This could be the TDP or some percentage of it. You won't be able to calculate your true carbon footprint, but if you hold this value constant, you can still calculate relative increases or decreases in $CO_2e$ as you change the other two factors in the kWh formula (the number of processors and the number of hours they run).

The second number we need, the average carbon emissions per kWh, is built into the US Environmental Protection Agency (EPA) Greenhouse Gas Equivalencies Calculator (*https://oreil.ly/vX_g8*). Just plug in the kWh you calculated earlier (as in Figure 6-1) and see that the $CO_2e$ of 1,664 kWh is 0.72 metric tons. These emissions are roughly equivalent to those from driving a gasoline-powered car 1,845 miles (2,969 kilometers), which is about the distance from San Francisco, California, to Kansas City, Missouri, or a round trip between Paris and Rome. Keep in mind that these emissions calculations are based on US averages and will vary by data center.

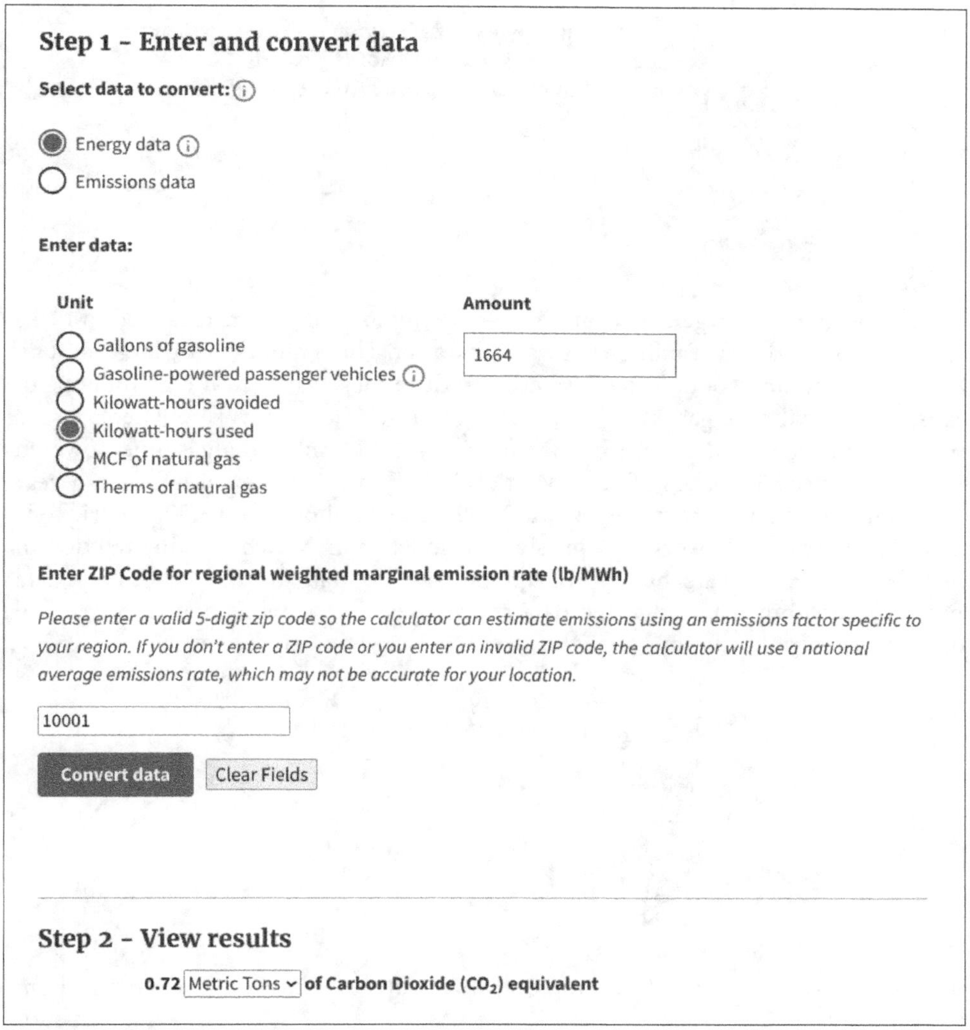

## Step 1 – Enter and convert data

**Select data to convert:** ⓘ

🔘 Energy data ⓘ
⚪ Emissions data

**Enter data:**

**Unit**

⚪ Gallons of gasoline
⚪ Gasoline-powered passenger vehicles ⓘ
⚪ Kilowatt-hours avoided
🔘 Kilowatt-hours used
⚪ MCF of natural gas
⚪ Therms of natural gas

**Amount**

1664

**Enter ZIP Code for regional weighted marginal emission rate (lb/MWh)**

*Please enter a valid 5-digit zip code so the calculator can estimate emissions using an emissions factor specific to your region. If you don't enter a ZIP code or you enter an invalid ZIP code, the calculator will use a national average emissions rate, which may not be accurate for your location.*

10001

[ **Convert data** ]  [ Clear Fields ]

## Step 2 – View results

**0.72** [ Metric Tons ⌄ ] **of Carbon Dioxide (CO$_2$) equivalent**

*Figure 6-1. The EPA's Greenhouse Gas Equivalencies Calculator*

> These carbon numbers you've shown so far seem pretty small to me. It sounds like we don't have much of an emissions problem.

Let's up the game. A large data center may have millions of servers arranged in racks and drawing hundreds of millions of watts of power. These numbers are large enough that I'll stop talking about kilowatts and introduce megawatts (MW), or millions of watts. The greenhouse gas emissions from 1 megawatt hour (MWh) of energy use is roughly equivalent to the emissions from driving 1,100 miles in a gasoline-powered car or burning 485 pounds of coal. Multiply that by the number of hours in a year (365 × 24), and now we're talking about 8,760 megawatt hours and 3,800 metric tons of $CO_2$e. That's a year's worth of emissions from 843 cars, which is a tiny fraction of the world's 1+ billion cars, but it's not zero either. And that's just one year in one data center. I'm assuming here that the data center uses electricity generated from fossil fuels, however, which might not be the case. I'll discuss this more later.

> So, basically, my code has a carbon footprint and I can measure it.

That's right. And I've been measuring only one source of emissions. Let's expand on that.

# Beyond Direct Carbon Emissions

*I hear chatter about "scope 1" and "scope 2" carbon emissions. What's that?*

People who are deep into the research on greenhouse gas emissions separate them into three categories or *scopes*:

*Scope 1*

This includes direct emissions to the environment from *stuff you own*. An example is the emissions from burning fuel in your car or emissions from your air conditioner refrigerant leaking. (Note that the latter has higher global warming potential than plain old $CO_2$, so please fix any leaks pronto!)

*Scope 2*

This includes emissions from energy *you purchase to run your stuff*. These emissions are associated with generating the energy you use for everything from running your lights to charging your phone. If you're a company, your scope 2 emissions are related to the electricity you purchase to run your business, whether it's for a small office or a giant data center.

*Scope 3*

This includes everything else, such as emissions associated with your supply chain. If you make and sell stuff, this also includes the emissions associated with using and transporting your products. The scope 3 emissions of most businesses likely dwarf their scope 1 and 2 emissions. Google's 2023 environmental report, for example, says that "Scope 3 emissions represent 75% of our carbon footprint" (*https://oreil.ly/5qEjm*).

**Measuring Carbon Emissions** | 139

So hey, do you make phones? Then the electricity someone uses to charge their phone is in your scope 3 and also in *their* scope 2. Did you just buy a server? The electricity and direct emissions associated with making that server are in your scope 3 and in the supply chain's scope 1 and 2. Do you drive to work? The emissions associated with your car burning gas are in your scope 1 and the fuel company's scope 3. If this all seems complicated, you're not alone in thinking that, but the goal is to help businesses understand their direct and indirect emissions so they can focus on reducing both.

# Controlling Your Code's Carbon Footprint

Electricity-related emissions from data centers are just part of the total $CO_2e$ associated with software, but they offer a great opportunity for carbon savings. As a software engineer, you can help out by changing your code and managing your servers to use less energy or cleaner energy. Let's discuss three primary areas where you may have control over your systems' emissions:

*Processor usage*
How many processors do you use, and how much time do you use them for?

*Location*
Which data centers run your code?

*Time of day*
During which hours of the day does your code run?

## Controlling Processor Usage

If your code runs in a data center, it probably runs on multiple processors. But how many does it need? This number is generally under your (or your team's) control, and if you reduce it, you can reduce $CO_2e$. Here are three general approaches you could take and which I'll discuss in turn:

- Code optimizations, such as more efficient algorithms
- More efficient allocation of computing resources (CPUs, disk, and memory)
- Running code on Tensor Processing Units (TPUs) and graphics processing units (GPUs) when appropriate

Optimizations in your code can change your carbon footprint. We know this from firsthand experience at Google. Even tiny reductions in processing, like copying strings more quickly in memory, can produce huge gains in energy efficiency when scaled across Google's massive operations. Googlers who create the most impactful optimizations even receive awards called Perfy Awards. (No cash, just bragging rights.)

*I like the sound of that, but I own a lot of code. How do I figure out what to optimize?*

A great way to optimize your code is to focus your attention on the most expensive functions: those that use the most CPU time or are called most often. To locate these potential performance hogs, use a *code profiler*: a tool that runs your code and computes statistics about function calls. The "Mini Case Study: Profiling an Application" sidebar presents an example of a code profiler. Once you've isolated the most expensive functions, try to optimize them. This could mean changing an algorithm or porting the functions to a higher performance language. At Google, when we write Python applications, for example, we've been known to rewrite the frequently executed functions in C++ for greater performance.

Be aware of the trade-off between optimizing your code and keeping it easy to read and understand. Too much optimization can produce convoluted code and lead to more and tougher bugs, which will waste developer time and increase maintenance costs. Also beware of optimizing too early, since your code may behave very differently (with a different carbon footprint) on your development computer than in a data center. As the famous hacker saying goes, "Premature optimization is the root of all evil" (*https://oreil.ly/7AM4W*).

# Mini Case Study: Profiling an Application

Years ago, when I was a software engineer at a previous company, our ecommerce website started having performance issues shortly after a software update. Pages were loading slowly, and our customers were affected. I was the lucky engineer on call that week, so it fell to me to figure out what was going on. Our application contained millions of lines of code, so there was no way I (or anyone else) could eyeball the code and find the problem. So, I fired up a code profiler, loaded in the whole web application, and let it run in a test environment.

The profiler quickly revealed that one particular function, which I'll call `function A`, was accounting for almost 90% of the execution time, which was not normal. In pseudocode, the function looked something like this:

```
function A(int limit) {
  i = 0;
  while (i < limit) {
    B(i++);
  }
}
```

I didn't think `function A` looked suspicious, but it did repeatedly call a second function, which I'll call `function B`:

```
function B() {
  ⋮
  if (condition) {
    Log.Write(debug_message);
  }
}
```

The problem was now clear. Our application was writing millions of debugging messages to the server log file. This was killing performance because (1) something had caused the `condition` variable in `function B` to be true most of the time, (2) appending to a log file is a slow operation, and (3) the log writes were happening inside of a loop. So, we removed the call to `Log.Write` and our application sped up by a factor of 10. An (extremely apologetic) engineer had inserted the `Log.Write` call for debugging and forgotten to remove it before launch.

Thanks to the code profiler, we isolated a performance problem in minutes instead of hours or days. In my experience, profilers are one of the least appreciated tools for software engineers. I'm constantly surprised by how many developers—even engineers with decades of experience—rarely or never use them. I promise they are worth the time to learn, and the speedups you'll achieve can lead to reduced $CO_2e$ and increased efficiency. Search the web for the name of your preferred programming language followed by `code profiler` to locate tools for your use.

Besides code optimization, look for opportunities to reduce the computing resources that are allocated to your application, such as processors, memory, and disk space. This technique is called *capacity management*.

Suppose your web application receives double its usual traffic on holidays. For this sort of seasonal application, you might be tempted to allocate CPUs to handle peak capacity and leave them in place all the time, just in case of load spikes. But that would mean on nonholidays, which is most of the year, half of your fleet of CPUs might be sitting idle, wasting energy (and money!), and producing unnecessary $CO_2e$. A good cloud provider will provide an API or dashboard to measure these sorts of wasted resources, such as the idle time of your CPUs, unused RAM, and unallocated disk space. (How many years' worth of log files are you storing? How many do you really need?) Use that data to thoughtfully manage your applications' various capacities.

Beyond code optimizations and capacity management, keep your eyes open for CPU processing that would be more efficient on other kinds of processors, such as a graphics processing unit (GPU) or an optimized AI chip such as a TPU. GPUs tend to use more energy than CPUs, but they're much faster for certain tasks, like image and video processing, so their total energy consumption may be less overall than a CPU's. TPUs, on the other hand, are *much* more energy and speed efficient than CPUs. They're optimized for training ML models. (Don't train an ML model on CPUs if you can help it!) Your applications can achieve huge savings in speed, energy, and $CO_2e$ with the right processing units.

## What About Coding for Performance?

> As an engineer, I love optimizing my code and database queries to shave milliseconds off my runtime. How is performance optimization related to emissions?

Optimizations that reduce CPU cycles, RAM, disk space, and network traffic generally also reduce $CO_2e$. Go for it!

Optimizations that just make your code run in less time, however, may or may not decrease $CO_2e$. It depends on *how* you reduced the runtime. Did you write a cleverer algorithm and run it on the same hardware? Then yes, that's likely to reduce $CO_2e$ by reducing CPU cycles. Did you speed things up by adding more servers? Then your

$CO_2e$ could increase because it's running on more physical CPUs, even if it occupies them for less time. The calculation gets more complicated as CPUs gain many more cores, because computing with many cores in a single chip is typically very energy efficient.

Another decent measure of $CO_2e$ reduction, if you host your code with a third-party cloud provider, is cost. Look at the invoice you receive and pay each billing period. Higher cost generally means higher resource use and therefore higher $CO_2e$. If you optimize your code and your cost drops, then you've probably reduced $CO_2e$ too. Finally, check whether your cloud provider has a tool for estimating $CO_2e$, such as Google Cloud's Carbon Footprint tool (*https://oreil.ly/sDNMq*).

## Controlling the Code's Location

*All cloud providers are pretty much the same these days, right? My company just uses the cheapest one.*

Running code in the cloud is, on average, more energy efficient than running it on premises—but all providers are not the same. Specifically, *where does your provider get its electricity*? Its local electrical grid might produce electricity by burning fossil fuels, which is a carbon-intensive technique—or it might include renewable energy sources, like hydroelectric, solar, and wind, which have very low or no carbon emissions. The greener a data center, the more intensively you can use its computing resources with less environmental impact.

To display the climate impact of electricity in specific regions of the world, check out *app.electricitymaps.com*. Your cloud provider may also publish summary statistics for its data centers or regions, such as Google Cloud's carbon data across Google Cloud Platform (GCP) regions (*https://oreil.ly/rVCIJ*).

Besides $CO_2e$, cloud providers may publish other metrics as points of comparison, which may help you to choose a relatively green provider. Here are a few metrics from a Google research paper (*https://oreil.ly/xef60*):

*Carbon intensity*

This is the number of tons of $CO_2e$ per megawatt hour. This metric tells you how *clean* a data center is—that is, how low or high its emissions are. Lower values are greener.

*Power usage effectiveness (PUE)*

This is the center's total energy use divided by the amount consumed by its computing hardware. This tells you how *efficient* a data center is with its energy. When PUE equals 1.1, for example (which happens to be Google's average PUE in its data centers at press time (*https://oreil.ly/mrwuo*)), it means for every megawatt consumed by computing hardware, another 10% is spent elsewhere to operate the data center. Lower values are greener.

*Carbon-free energy percentage (%CFE)*

This is the percentage of energy used by the data center that comes from carbon-free sources, such as wind and solar power. The %CFE tells you how *green* a data center is. Higher values are greener. One hundred percent would mean zero $CO_2$ emissions.

Even a single provider's data centers may vary quite a bit when it comes to their sustainability. For example, the cloud services offered by Amazon Web Services (*https://oreil.ly/MfKzl*), Google Cloud (*https://oreil.ly/Tw1Sq*), and Microsoft Azure (*https://oreil.ly/46K-y*) are hosted in dozens of regions around the world—spanning hundreds of countries with different norms, practices, and laws regarding the environment. If your cloud provider supports it, choose to run your code in the provider's greener data centers. If your provider doesn't publish enough information on this topic, ask for it. Let them know that, as a paying customer, you require this data in order to make good decisions.

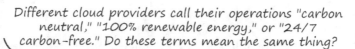

Different cloud providers call their operations "carbon neutral," "100% renewable energy," or "24/7 carbon-free." Do these terms mean the same thing?

These terms are a hot topic, and experts are still debating how and when to use them. Nevertheless, let's take a crack at their possible meanings at a high level.

*Carbon neutral* often means that the provider is buying credits, called carbon offsets, that reduce or prevent emissions globally. The reduced emissions may not necessarily be their own. If the total credits they purchase equal their own carbon footprint, they may say they are carbon neutral. *100% renewable energy* usually means the provider is purchasing renewable energy in large enough quantities to match its annual electricity use, but they also may still have some carbon emissions. Finally, *24/7 carbon-free* generally means the provider has addressed its emissions by sourcing clean energy for every hour of every day, in every grid where it operates. As an example, as of 2022, Google has matched 100% of the electricity consumption of its global operations with purchases of renewable energy annually since 2017. Google has also set a goal to address its scope 2 emissions associated with operational electricity use by 2030, by running on 24/7 carbon-free energy on every grid where it operates (making it 24/7 carbon-free for scope 2). This goal presents many opportunities and challenges because data centers run increasingly large and complex AI code, energy policies differ around the world, and clean energy itself can be complex to generate and transmit.

## Optimizing for Time of Day

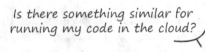

Data centers may use different sources of power at different times of day. You may be able to reduce your $CO_2e$ by running your code at times when low-carbon power is plentiful. This is particularly true for relatively large jobs, like training an ML model, which can take days or weeks and may not be time-sensitive. Schedule these jobs to run at low-emissions times for the local grid.

One caveat: as technology improves, data centers are becoming smarter at scheduling jobs to run efficiently. Within Google, for example, software called the Carbon-Intelligent Computing System automatically delays certain compute tasks so they run during less carbon-intensive times of day, based on predictions about the electrical grid (*https://oreil.ly/1e1ab*). Your cloud provider may already be taking into account the time of day to reduce its costs. Ask your provider whether your own time-of-day optimizations would be helpful or if you should let its scheduling algorithms choose when to run your non-time-sensitive code.

# Getting Involved

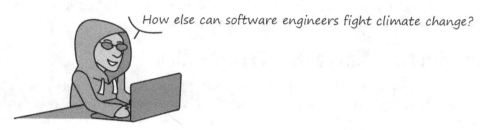

Even if we reduce or eliminate data center emissions from our own code, the world still has plenty of other climate change–related problems to solve. By and large, technologists like us love solving problems. So what else can we do?

A great start is to join climate change–related projects where your technology skills can help. In the world of open source, GitHub maintains a list of climate change projects (*https://oreil.ly/OroDX*), and last time I looked, there were over one thousand projects listed. Also, check out the Green Software Foundation (*https://oreil.ly/w-BEE*), whose mission is "to reduce the total change in global carbon emissions associated with software."

Closer to home, if you're lucky, your employer might have an interest in such projects, especially if you work in Big Tech. Google, for example, has a sizable community of employees, called Anthropocene, who are passionate about mitigating climate change and its effects. Twice a year, it holds a "climate fair" and invites all Googlers to learn about dozens of climate-related projects and join as volunteers. I had the privilege of working on two such projects. The first was Project Sunroof (*https://oreil.ly/YLPg8*), which calculates the costs and energy savings of rooftop solar panels at a given street address. It uses Google Maps APIs to render the intensity of sunlight on rooftops. I started out by updating Sunroof documentation but soon transitioned to a related project, the Environmental Insights Explorer (*https://oreil.ly/Mol_h*). This project provides greenhouse gas data to city governments so they can make informed decisions to reduce emissions. I had the opportunity to write software for the project on a small and enthusiastic team for a few hours a week.

If your company doesn't have anything similar to Anthropocene, then consider starting a special interest group yourself (if it makes sense, given your role and the company's size and mission). It's been my experience that most engineers "get it" about climate change and want to help; all they need is an opportunity. Also, talk to your management about reducing carbon or steering its business toward greener data centers. Saving energy usually means saving money. And if your company produces hardware, advocate for it to be repairable instead of throw-away-and-replace.

If you happen to work for a cloud provider or in a data center, check whether your employer publicizes its green statistics, such as carbon intensity, PUE, and %CFE. If not, consider whether it would benefit your business to provide these statistics to customers. Greener operations can give you a competitive edge.

## Case Study: Cooling a Data Center with AI

AI programming is sometimes blamed for extreme processing loads in data centers. This case study flips that story around to show how AI can be applied responsibly to save energy.

In the mid-2010s, Google was using lots of energy to cool its data centers. Curious Googlers began to wonder: could we save energy by controlling the temperature of our data centers with AI? Not long before, Google's DeepMind division had created an AI application called AlphaGo that could beat human players at the board game Go. Could Google apply similar ML technology to beat humans at the game of climate control?

Data center cooling works like this (or at least it did at the time): Chilled water is pumped into the data center to cool the building. The water warms in the process and is pumped to a chiller, which extracts the heat from the water and vents the heat elsewhere, and the process repeats.

Other companies had previously tried and failed to cool hardware with AI to optimize cost. This time was different, however, because of the AlphaGo team's expertise in a branch of ML called deep reinforcement learning.

Intuitively, *reinforcement learning* (RL) is like learning by trial and error. Good decisions by the AI are rewarded and poor ones are penalized, according to some mathematical function. If all goes well, the AI converges on a set of rules of behavior that maximizes reward. This technique is popular for AI models that play games and solve puzzles. Little by little, the system moves its game pieces incrementally closer to a win or a solution, and it learns which moves work well in which states.

*Deep reinforcement learning* is a variety of RL. It begins by creating a model of the world (in this case, a model of the data center) by examining gobs of real-world data and applying supervised ML.[3] Once the model is ready, the RL system is told to begin in some state, and it makes its first prediction. Then, a software agent looks at the prediction and takes action by moving the model to a different state that, ideally,

---

3 Technically, this is model-based RL. Not all RL systems use a model.

148 | Chapter 6: Measuring and Reducing Your Code's Carbon Footprint

improves upon the previous state. This process repeats, the system progresses from state to state, and the agent gradually learns which actions work best in which states. The best outcome is for the RL system to reach a stable state or *set point*, such as an ideal temperature range for data center machinery, and to maintain that set point over time.

This process is tricky. If you're not careful, the RL system can produce trivial results. The agent could learn, for example, that the ideal state is to shut off cooling altogether—which will produce unbeatable energy savings while your chips melt. The system also needs to compensate for real-world constraints. Turning chillers on and off frequently is expensive and can wear out the machinery.

To tackle these challenges, Google assembled a team that included, at first, software engineers, AlphaGo research scientists, and mechanical engineers who design data centers. The team created a very simple, low-budget prototype, all duct tape and bubble gum. The AI system would issue predictions of set points for the cooling system, and the team would email the predictions to real-live humans in the data center. If the system's recommendation seemed reasonable, the humans would implement it by tweaking the cooling controls.

The cheap prototype worked pretty well, so in the next phase of the project, the team traveled to the data center and tested the system live. By colocating with the data center personnel, the engineers learned about complex interactions among machines in the data center, which were not apparent from the data and which their model did not cover. (Recall from Chapter 3 that production systems can be way more complex than development and testing systems.) The team learned a ton, saved time, and avoided all kinds of hiccups. In the end, the system reduced the energy used for data center cooling by up to 40% (*https://oreil.ly/eFH43*)! This was a significant energy savings.

Once the system seemed to be stable and operating well, the team asked: what would happen if full control was turned over to the AI? (Cue dramatic music.) The team couldn't be sure, so it carefully built a safety mechanism. This mechanism was based on constraints defined by Google's data center operators. The software engineers programmed the safety mechanism so that the safety mechanism wouldn't trust the AI and the AI wouldn't trust the safety mechanism. This is called a *mutual distrust model*. If the two systems disagreed about a recommendation, then they would throw it away. Plus, at all times, human operators could override the AI.

The resulting AI-controlled cooling system worked well enough for Google to implement it across a number of its data centers. In fact, it was one of the first major successes of RL ever deployed in the real world. Over time, the system has delivered significant, consistent energy savings.

Let's review the factors that make the data center cooling solution a great example of responsible software engineering:

*A responsible goal*
Reduced cooling costs translate into reduced carbon emissions.

*Cross-functional collaboration*
The software engineers worked closely with research scientists from AlphaGo and the boots-on-the-ground workers in the data center. This arrangement simplified collaboration and built trust among professionals with different skill sets.

*Focus on safety*
The team kept a human expert in the loop to carry out and then confirm the AI's commands. Eventually, control was handed to the AI, but only after the team created a mutual distrust model that would discard potentially risky recommendations.

Following Google's lead, various companies today offer AI-based products for climate control in data centers. The problem is not yet fully solved, however, because solutions do not scale well from one data center to another. Many data centers have unique setups: they contain different equipment, and they generate and collect different data in different formats. As one Google engineer told me, "The biggest roadblock to mitigating climate change with AI is data standardization." The AI itself is relatively well-understood at this point. What's harder is getting the data into the right format at a large scale. This is an area of active research.

## Summary

Everyone can reduce their carbon footprint in all sorts of ways, like using less gasoline. Those of us with software development skills can do even more. Start by measuring your code's carbon footprint. If you don't have enough data to measure it effectively, advocate for your data centers to provide what you need. Once you understand your footprint, you can work to reduce it. And if you have time, consider getting involved in coding projects to mitigate climate change. The work can be deeply satisfying, and the ultimate goal is critical for our planet.

# CHAPTER 7
# Building a Culture of Responsible Software Engineering

All the topics I've covered so far—mitigating bias, incorporating societal context, planning for unintended consequences, preserving privacy, reducing your code's carbon footprint, and the rest—only matter if they're put into practice.

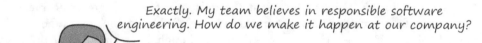

*Exactly. My team believes in responsible software engineering. How do we make it happen at our company?*

If you want to implement responsible software engineering for your business, it's a multipart challenge:

*Setting policy*
What *kinds* of responsible software engineering should you value and practice?

*Spreading the word*
How do you *alert and educate* coworkers, and what kinds of resistance might you meet?

*Following responsible processes*
What are *best practices* for bringing a product from idea to launch responsibly?

*Creating incentives*
How can you *smooth the way* for people to make responsible choices?

*Learning from mistakes*
How do you *prevent errors of the past* from being forgotten and repeated?

*Measuring success*
How can you *know* if you're being responsible?

One important word you'll see in this chapter is *governance*. It means setting up and enforcing a system of rules and processes within an organization. Responsible software engineering definitely benefits from strong governance, such as communicating the company's responsible goals broadly, creating a responsible launch process for products, and establishing committees or panels for oversight.

In this chapter, I'll assume you work for a company that would benefit from more responsible practices. If you're trying to create a culture of responsible software engineering from scratch, a big question is whether or not you're in a position of power to make changes. I'll offer suggestions both for leaders and for those of us who are further from the top. On the other hand, if you're lucky enough to work for a company that already has some responsible practices in place, then this chapter may provide some new ideas to try out.

## Setting Policy

Way back in Chapter 1, I laid out what responsible software engineering means: developing software applications that are socially beneficial and don't harm the Earth or its inhabitants. This description is pretty broad, though. No team or company can do it all, and it may be impossible to satisfy every possible stakeholder (leadership, employees, customers, society, etc.). Your company may also define responsibility in all sorts of ways. So, the first question to ask is, what kind of responsible engineering does your company want to practice?

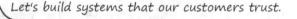
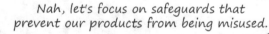
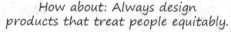

Some parts of responsible software engineering are must-haves because they're backed up by laws or regulations like the GDPR (see Chapter 5). Companies that do business internationally can't simply refuse to protect their users' privacy, unless they want to be socked with heavy fines. But many other aspects of responsibility are up to the practitioner.

## Sponsorship and Support

As I interviewed Googlers for this chapter, one message came through loud and clear: to build a culture of responsibility, you must have strong support from senior leadership. Your CEO needs to talk about it with employees and also publicly. Other leaders must be willing to consider long-term benefits over short-term ones, like slowing down product releases to implement and test them responsibly. Without this sort of executive support, employees may not realize (or believe) that responsible software engineering is an organizational priority.

I'll talk about changing minds in "Incentives from the Bottom Up" on page 165, but a useful way to begin is to frame the issues in terms of *quality* and *safety*. If your product can cause bad things to happen (meaning there's a safety issue), then at the very least, that's a bug (a quality issue) that can be triaged and addressed through your company's usual processes. Senior leaders know that quality and safety issues can cost the company money and customers, so these concepts may be more actionable for them than, say, ethical or moral concerns.

## Mini Case Study: Sharing the Customer Impact

In 2019, Ben Treynor Sloss had a realization. As a vice president at Google Cloud, he was proud that his software development teams had worked so hard to build and launch new features and increase Cloud's capacity. At the same time, Cloud had experienced multiple outages that had affected its customers' trust in the service. It seemed to Ben that his teams often heard about feature requests from product managers and pending deals from the sales division, but not nearly as much about product failures from Google's support teams.

Ben gathered everyone in Google's Cloud and Technical Infrastructure organizations for a mandatory meeting. He explained that Cloud had had a series of outages due to reliability issues, so he was going to show them some direct quotes from customers who had contacted Cloud about how they'd been affected. For the next 10 minutes, Ben presented a slide deck with page after page of emotional comments from individuals and businesses. They described how they relied on Cloud for their livelihoods. They spoke of how angry they'd been and how helpless they'd felt when Cloud had failed. The room was silent. ("You could hear a pin drop," Ben told me.)

Years after these events, I asked some Googlers who attended Ben's meeting to recall their reactions. Some were stunned by the customer comments. Some were angry that leadership seemed to be blaming engineers for systemic problems. Others, however, felt motivated by seeing a senior executive walking the walk and building empathy to solidify a culture of responsibility toward customers. "When *we* are down," Ben had said, "*they* are down." Ultimately, the meeting launched a new standard to prioritize reliability-related bugs over requests for new features, and Google Cloud's uptime improved significantly.

Alongside executive support, your company should establish power structures that uphold responsible software engineering practices. This is an important part of governance. Google DeepMind, for example, has a Responsibility and Safety Council that includes vice presidents, directors, and other area heads, as well as ethicists and social scientists. Some of the council members have responsible engineering as their main mandate, while others do not. The council reviews projects to ensure they're safe and in line with Google DeepMind's AI principles. Without appropriate power structures in place, you and your coworkers may have the best intentions to implement responsible engineering but may still be unable to do so.

## Misunderstandings About a Culture of Responsibility

Company culture is hard to change in general. Here are a few arguments you might encounter when drumming up support for responsible software engineering.

## "It's just branding."

"Responsible engineering" is just branding. Tech companies just want to look good to the public so they make more money.

I have to admit, I used to think that when companies promoted a "culture of responsibility," it was mostly lip service. But while I was researching this book, the people I talked to changed my mind. I met so many passionate individuals, from coders to executives, who really care about responsibility for its own sake because it's good for the world.

Really? Then why isn't more software engineered responsibly?

There isn't a single, simple reason, but here's a common one: software teams face many competing challenges, and responsible engineering is just one of them. A team's products also have to be secure from intruders, be maintainable so they can be improved, be scalable to millions of users, be configurable to please different audiences, have a flawless user interface that's translatable into many languages and accessible to users with disabilities, and be available at an affordable price that keeps the company in business. Oh yeah, and the products also have to *work*. No team can optimize for all of these factors at once. It has to make hard decisions that prioritize some factors over others—and sometimes, responsibility suffers.

Dozens of competing factors go into creating a product. Try to keep responsible software engineering in the top five to maintain a culture of responsibility.

Setting Policy | 155

As an aside, I've certainly met people in the tech industry who don't care about user privacy, carbon emissions, fair AI, and other aspects of responsibility—but in my experience, they are the exception rather than the rule.

## "It's just compliance."

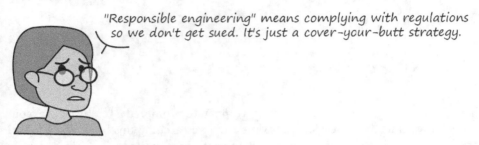

It's important to have regulations and laws to keep software safe and fair for customers. A great example is the "Click to Cancel" rule enacted by the US Federal Trade Commission in 2024. It requires any company that offers a subscription service to make cancellation as easy as the initial sign-up. Hooray!

But regulations and laws aren't the whole story. Most professionals I've met in the field of compliance don't like fixing problems after they occur. They'd much rather work with a software team in advance, during product design and development, to produce the best outcome that is also compliant.

## "It's just bureaucracy."

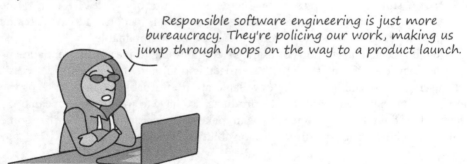

As a software engineer who has experienced plenty of pointless-seeming bureaucracy, I definitely empathize with this viewpoint! My experience has been, however, that these sorts of roadblocks often come from well-meaning people who may not realize the level of burden they're imposing on others. Whenever possible, I've engaged my curiosity and had conversations with the folks who were imposing the rules. In some cases, I've learned the reasoning behind the rules, which has made them seem less bureaucratic—or I've managed to communicate the pain that the rules have caused, which has led us to brainstorm better ways to accomplish the intended goal.

Also, if responsible engineering at your company feels like surveillance over your work, then that may be a sign of an ailing relationship. In my experience, a good compliance department doesn't want to be the ethics police—it wants to be a thought partner in a successful product launch. Try reaching out proactively in the earliest stages of your product development and partnering with a member of your compliance department. A strong relationship with them may smooth the road toward launch.

# Spreading the Word

Once you have obtained general support for responsible software engineering, the rest of the company needs to hear about it. Let's talk about how to make that happen.

## Messaging

If you want a whole company to understand and practice responsible software engineering, then start with a consistent vocabulary and share it. When members of your leadership team all use the same terminology and pass it down, the rest of the company will be more likely to adopt it. It's also fine to invent terms: when you create a word and share it, it becomes real. For example, you could call your most active advocates "responsible engineering champions." Establish a "carbon checkup" to measure a project's data center emissions. Use whatever vocabulary works within your corporate culture. Work those words into emails, newsletters, and other communications.

As an example within Google, the Engineering Education team (more on them later) creates and publishes a series of articles called "AI Smart Practices" that help build a shared understanding of responsible AI among Googlers. Some past article topics have included AI fairness, transparency, differential privacy, and child safety. An article on privacy, for example, taught Googlers how to think in general about privacy problems and specific ways to counter them, as we did in Chapter 5. The ultimate goal of these articles is to help Googlers build safe and reliable products that work for everyone.

We should create an intranet website that gathers all our information on responsible software engineering so our employees can find it.

A central clearinghouse for responsible software engineering information can be a great resource, and these sorts of sites are usually announced with great fanfare, but they're also surprisingly difficult to do well. Here are some best practices for a successful internal site:

*Going beyond the launch*
Even if your website has a gigantic rollout with balloons and circus animals, it'll be overlooked or forgotten over time, particularly as new people join the company. Point people toward the site frequently so it stays in their minds and continues to add value.

*Testing it carefully with your internal search engine*
Employees don't search your intranet for "responsible engineering info center" or whatever your VP named your website. They search for specific problems they need to solve in the moment. Make sure the topics on your website are indexed well by your company search engine.

*Testing it with generative AI*
If your company uses an AI to retrieve internal knowledge, ask it lots of questions about responsible software engineering to see if it pulls the right information from your website. If it doesn't, speak with your AI maintainers.

*Making updates easy*
Your website should be frictionless for adding and updating content. Correcting a typo should take less than 10 seconds; otherwise, people won't spend the time to do it, let alone make larger changes. Smooth the path for eager authors—don't force them to battle a site's infrastructure to contribute.

*Having a maintenance plan*
Time is the enemy of internal knowledge sites as their content silently becomes outdated. How will it stay current? The answer is to have motivated contributors for the long term.

Your company may also want to communicate outside its walls, with its customers and the world, about responsible software engineering. Google, for example, writes publicly about responsible software engineering for the public. Examples are its responsible AI policy (*https://oreil.ly/gd63I*), which is for a general audience, and its fairness in machine learning materials (*https://oreil.ly/RRPIz*), which are for a technical audience. These sorts of external communications can bolster your company's reputation.

# Educating New Hires

Even if your company regularly broadcasts about responsible software engineering, new hires may need more information about it to help bring them into the company culture. At Google, our technical orientation process introduces new Googlers (who are known as *Nooglers*) to responsible AI, responsible innovation, ethical decision making, user privacy, and the downstream consequences of releasing technology into the world. We base some Noogler training on a terrific research paper, "Developing a Framework for Responsible Innovation" (*https://oreil.ly/s-5Wf*), which suggests responsible questions that Googlers can ask about the products and processes they encounter.

Google DeepMind, an AI research lab, automatically enrolls new hires in a course on ethics and safety in which they actively discuss and debate ethical situations. Google DeepMind also runs a more advanced internal course called the AI Ethics in Practice Workshop. This daylong course was created and conducted in partnership with a group outside of Alphabet, and it guides learners through a variety of ethical dilemmas and safety questions. It's also structured around three sets of custom-made cards like the ones in Figure 7-1:

*Process cards*

These are cards that guide learners to evaluate a specific technology. The top left card in Figure 7-1, "Mitigations," is a process card. It's part of a five-step process to assess a technology by its benefits, risks, mitigation strategies, moral issues, and an overall assessment.

*Tool cards*

These are cards for tools that learners can apply, such as fact-finding, ethical pre- and post-mortems, and future regret (see Chapter 4). The top right card in Figure 7-1, "Expanding the ethical circle," is a tool card.

*Lenses*

These are cards for different perspectives the learners can take while grappling with moral issues. The card that's shown from the front and back at the bottom of Figure 7-1, "Common good," is a lens.

Using these cards, learners can think through the benefits, risks, mitigation strategies, and moral issues of specific technologies. For example, one way to mitigate a risk (as mentioned on the top left card of Figure 7-1) is to work more broadly with other people who may be impacted by that technology (as suggested on the top right card), and while doing so, we should consider the common good (the focus of the bottom card).

| **Mitigations** | **Expanding the ethical circle** |
|---|---|
| Is it possible to mitigate these risks, or eliminate them entirely? | Incorporating the perspectives of those impacted |
| How could these risks be mitigated (e.g., from technical, organizational, or policy perspectives)?<br><br>Are there scenarios where these mitigations may not work?<br><br>Which mitigations are feasible to implement now?<br><br>Which mitigations need more research? | Who will be most directly and indirectly affected by our project?<br><br>Who is at greatest risk of harm, and how?<br><br>Have we made assumptions about people instead of consulting them?<br><br>How do we engage these groups? |

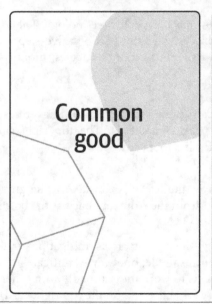

| | How do we cultivate the conditions that are required in order for all members of a society to flourish?<br><br>How do we build and preserve the shared institutions needed for a healthy society? |
|---|---|

*Figure 7-1. A process card (at the top left), a tool card (at the top right), and a lens card (on the bottom, shown front and back) adapted from the AI Ethics in Practice Workshop run by Google DeepMind*

160 | Chapter 7: Building a Culture of Responsible Software Engineering

Interested in trying something similar? The AI Ethics in Practice Workshop has implemented portions of another toolkit that's available under a Creative Commons license. It's called *Ethics in Tech Practice: A Toolkit* (*https://oreil.ly/yQhN2*), and it's from the Markkula Center for Applied Ethics at Santa Clara University. Check it out if you want to design an ethics workshop of your own.

# Establishing Processes

Educating your coworkers is all well and good, but to change your company culture, you also need to *practice* responsible software engineering. To do that, you need repeatable processes and some form of governance to make sure people follow them.

> I like having a process to follow, but who owns it? Does governance belong to a development team or a separate counterpart? Who's responsible for responsibility?

Ownership depends on how big your company is and how many things you need to do. At a small company with a single software development team, the team might be the right owner (as long as the team members consult with other experts in departments like legal, compliance, and so on). A large corporation might have one central governance organization or separate governance within each independent business unit.

A company's most important governance process for responsible software engineering, arguably, is the review process to verify that a product can be launched safely into the world. Ideally, product teams evaluate their products continuously, from the time they're brainstormed on a whiteboard to the time they're code complete. Even if that happens, it pays to have a consistent, repeatable review process that can catch issues the team may miss.

Google's review process for responsible AI (at press time) consists of four stages:

1. *Intake*
   Requesting a review

2. *Analysis*
   Investigating the product's potential benefits and harms

*3. Adjustment*
  Evaluating the product's safety

*4. Decision*
  Producing or abandoning the product

Let's consider the fictional project from Chapter 3, SpeekSplendid, which analyzes a person's presentation style via AI and offers users tips for improvement.

During the intake stage, the SpeekSplendid development team would request a review from their company's central AI principles (AIP) team. To prepare, the AIP team would review current AI research and similar products.

Then, during the analysis stage, the AIP team might consider the societal context (as detailed in Chapter 3) for SpeekSplendid and produce a list of questions like these, which draw attention to potential risks like those in the case study in Chapter 4:

- Can cheap webcams reliably capture the audio analysis?
- Could speakers with certain accents become stigmatized?
- What happens if the user base grows enormously?
- How will the company handle unexpected issues after launch?

In the adjustment stage, the AIP team would recommend specific tests for the risks they listed and estimate how often the risks are likely to happen in the real world.

Finally, in the decision stage, the AIP team would give the product a thumbs-up or thumbs-down, at least for its current implementation.

Clearly, nobody wants to build a product and have it shut down by a review team, so this kind of review process should start as early as possible, before implementation. The SpeekSplendid team can of course revise the product design to mitigate concerns that come up during review.

Google products also go through other reviews before launch, such as privacy reviews (which determine whether user data is being handled appropriately), security reviews (which determine whether the product can be hacked), and legal reviews (which determine whether the product complies with laws in the locations where it's available).

> ### Mini Case Study: Launching AI Portrait Light
>
> On Google's Pixel phone, the Pixel Camera and Google Photos apps can enhance photographs by adding artificial light. This feature, called AI Portrait Light, was a difficult technical challenge, especially for photos of people. If a person's skin in a photo appears dark, then the algorithm must figure out whether it's due to dim lighting or the person having a naturally darker skin tone. AI-based light-generating algorithms, according to Google, have traditionally struggled to distinguish these two cases from each other (*https://oreil.ly/CN3OM*). The AI Portrait Light team needed its algorithm to perform well to pass its launch review.
>
> A typical way to solve this kind of problem is to train the AI model on millions of portrait photos of people with different skin tones, with each portrait presented alone and with highly precise lighting so the AI model can learn effectively. That's a tremendous amount of data to gather or create, so instead, the product team tried something clever. The team algorithmically combined the faces of 70 individuals "with a broad range of skin tones [...] genders, face shapes, face proportions, and hairstyles." With this technique, the team generated millions of synthetic portrait photos to train its model and produce realistic lighting on a wide variety of skin tones (*https://oreil.ly/QeoWC*). AI Portrait Light is an example of an application that improved when a company launch process was in place.

Another way to build and enforce repeatable processes is through automation. You could use automation to check products and code for responsible practices or compliance with your company policies; to generate test cases for bias in applications (see "Counterfactual fairness" on page 27); or anywhere else that might bring benefit. If you're a software engineer, I'm sure you're already familiar with automation and don't need to be sold on its benefits, so go forth and automate!

# Creating Incentives

How can you inspire coworkers to take responsible software engineering seriously? The answer depends on how much power you have in your company. Let's explore some incentives to try from the top and bottom of the corporate hierarchy.

## Incentives from the Top Down

When leadership has a strong, long-term commitment to a product, then safety and responsibility become obvious investments. People who design suspension bridges are invested in their quality and longevity. Same thing if you're designing software that you want to be around in 5–10 years, not just three months. If you have the power to make change in your company, here are some ways to proceed.

The most important thing is to equip your team members with the resources and tools they need to do their work responsibly. If you skip this step, all the other incentives in the world won't matter.

From there, hire a director of responsibility and safety. Pay their team members well. Treat them like they're protecting your company's assets and they're as important as your engineering leads.

Keep track of how much pain your company suffers when your products fail because of a responsible software engineering issue. Major escalations are costly, and they sacrifice your customers' all-important trust.

Run a hackathon where your software engineers compete to build the best prototype of a responsible software product or feature. Implement the winning ideas and celebrate the winners.

Establish a company-wide award for responsible software engineering. Calculate how much money the winning ideas saved or made for your company and give the winners a percentage of that amount as a bonus.

> Meh.... We shouldn't coddle our employees. Just make responsible engineering a mandatory part of performance evaluations. That'll work!

It may be tempting to enforce responsible software engineering through performance evaluations. Just penalize people who fall short, right? This approach sometimes appeals to senior executives, but it doesn't seem to work well in practice. The average employee doesn't memorize their job requirements or whatever rubric your company may use to evaluate employees at the end of the year. They just try to get their work done. In my experience, it's better (and easier) to excite software engineers about responsible engineering by helping them understand what it's for—and what happens when they skip it—as long as they're given the time and support to succeed at it. Prefer carrots to sticks and reward employees who follow responsible software practices.

## Incentives from the Bottom Up

If you have no official power to drive change in your company, then it's harder to influence others, but you can still do it. Here are some ideas on how to incentivize your coworkers to practice responsible software engineering.

Tell stories. When other companies in your industry make errors of responsibility and are blasted in *The New York Times* or *The Wall Street Journal* (or viral posts), bring the news to the attention of your company's decision makers. If your company's products have similar risks that (luckily) haven't been discovered by the press yet, speak up internally. If you can't reach your leaders' ears, begin with your manager or start a constructive conversation on your company's messaging platform about the risks and possible solutions.

If your team doesn't have the time, support, or other resources to build software responsibly, let decision makers know. Focus your arguments on quality and safety, as I discussed earlier in "Sponsorship and Support" on page 153. Remind your leaders how important it is to protect the assets that you're working so hard to build.

You can also push for (and volunteer to run) some of the top-down incentives from the preceding section, like a responsible-engineering hackathon.

## An Ethical Dilemma

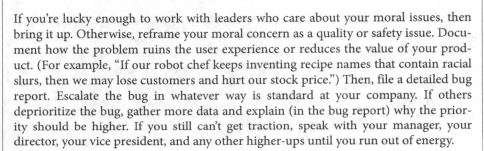

*My company doesn't have a culture of responsible engineering, and I've been asked to build something I morally disagree with. What now?*

If you're lucky enough to work with leaders who care about your moral issues, then bring it up. Otherwise, reframe your moral concern as a quality or safety issue. Document how the problem ruins the user experience or reduces the value of your product. (For example, "If our robot chef keeps inventing recipe names that contain racial slurs, then we may lose customers and hurt our stock price.") Then, file a detailed bug report. Escalate the bug in whatever way is standard at your company. If others deprioritize the bug, gather more data and explain (in the bug report) why the priority should be higher. If you still can't get traction, speak with your manager, your director, your vice president, and any other higher-ups until you run out of energy.

*What if that doesn't work?*

If others won't listen, then you may need to let the system fail and wait for *The New York Times*' exposé. Then, have a solution ready for when your leaders are finally ready to listen to you. Alternatively, find a new job that makes responsible software engineering a bigger priority.

# Learning from Mistakes

If, despite your best efforts, your systems still produce unwanted downstream consequences, then the next best thing (besides fixing the problem) is to learn from failure. At Google, when a production system fails, there's a strong expectation that the owning team will write and share an in-depth document, called a *postmortem*, that describes what happened and how we can prevent it in the future. Postmortems do not place blame; they turn mistakes into opportunities for learning. Googlers by and large consider a polished and insightful postmortem to be a respected accomplishment. Every engineer is one typo away from erasing the wrong filesystem or dropping a database by accident, and if a postmortem can prevent such mistakes from recurring, then it's valuable. In Chapter 3, I discussed an example of a Google postmortem for Jigsaw's Perspective API. The initial version of the API had labeled ordinary comments as toxic. The engineers at Jigsaw conducted a careful postmortem, which led to big improvements.

Encourage the teams in your company to create postmortems and make them blameless. Then, collect them into a *failure library* and encourage all employees to read them. Celebrate the people who contribute detailed analyses or postmortems to the library. Also, consider adding write-ups from outside your company that analyze high-profile, public failures. (Failure is expensive, so it pays to learn from everyone you can.)

Blameless postmortems and a failure library can help prevent the same safety mistake from happening twice. They're also great resources during tabletop exercises that simulate disasters (like the ones we discussed in Chapter 4). At Google, we found that a well-adopted postmortem process drove changes in our products and services that benefited users and the bottom line.

## Measuring Success

Does all this education and process change actually work?

It's very difficult to draw a straight line from a training course to an improvement in responsible engineering or a decrease in incidents or bugs. It's more realistic to measure lots of smaller or weaker factors and see if, together, they point toward positive results. Here are some examples of how to do this:

*Measure awareness or knowledge.*
Create quizzes or surveys that test whether your coworkers understand responsible engineering principles or at least are aware of them. I'll provide an example in the case study at the end of this chapter.

*Measure changes in carbon footprint.*
Use some techniques from Chapter 6 to demonstrate that your software is using less energy or cleaner energy.

*Measure engagement by product teams.*
How often do product teams work with responsibility-related teams, such as Compliance? How many teams are proactively approaching the responsibility-related team for help, versus the responsibility-related team reaching out to them first? Do product teams ask for guidance and thought partnership when their project begins (good), ask for a product review only toward the end (not great), or call in a panic after a launch goes badly (the worst)?

*Monitor external sentiment.*
Ask your customers what words come to mind when they describe your product or your company. Google DeepMind has done this, for example, and historically, its customers have mentioned the word *responsibility*. That's a good sign.

*Count incidents.*
How many responsibility-related scandals have you had relative to your competitors? What have these incidents cost you (and them)? Are your costs increasing or decreasing due to your efforts?

*Measure use of your failure library.*
Are teams making use of postmortems? Did they help the teams successfully avoid problems of the past?

Finally, create reports for your company leaders that display statistics like these. If you see positive trends, they'll suggest that you're building a culture of responsibility.

# Case Study: The Responsible Innovation Challenge

In 2018, Google published a set of AI Principles: responsible objectives for all Google-built AI applications. The principles stated at the time that AI applications should be or do the following things:[1]

1. Be socially beneficial
2. Avoid creating or reinforcing unfair bias
3. Be built and tested for safety
4. Be accountable to people
5. Incorporate privacy design principles

---

1 In 2025, Google updated its AI Principles (*https://oreil.ly/iLEnB*).

6. Uphold high standards of scientific excellence
7. Be made available for uses that accord with these principles

Stating these principles was a good first step for Google. The next step was to make sure Google's software engineers knew and understood the principles. That task fell to Google's Engineering Education (EngEDU) team. It formed a Responsible AI team to teach the AI Principles and evangelize responsible practices throughout the company.

The Responsible AI team first wondered, do our engineers already know the AI Principles? The team interviewed a number of Googlers who had completed some ML training courses (also created by EngEDU) and asked them if they knew the principles. The team found, to their surprise and dismay, that not a single person it polled could name or describe a single principle in any detail. At best, Google engineers were vaguely aware that Google had a bunch of AI Principles.

Life handed lemons to EngEDU's Responsible AI team, and it decided to make lemonade. It created a short, humorous video of an interviewer speaking with Googlers, one after another, asking if they could name an AI Principle. Each scene was like the one in Figure 7-2: one of the principles was very obviously displayed in the background—in giant letters on the side of a building, in the sky attached to an airplane, on all the T-shirts of a crowd, etc.—but the interviewed Googler couldn't name it. The video's ironic, tongue-in-cheek style was a hit within Google, with over 40,000 views, and it helped to teach Googlers the AI Principles, turning a seeming failure into a success.

*Figure 7-2. A scene from Google's internal video on its 2018 AI Principles*

Case Study: The Responsible Innovation Challenge | 169

It takes more than one video to reach tens of thousands of Google software engineers, so EngEDU's Responsible AI team developed more training materials. The next was a personality quiz called "Which AI Principle Are You?" Googlers filled out a questionnaire with some silly questions (such as picking your favorite beverage and snack) and some serious ones (pick a Google value and a responsible AI practice), and at the end, they received a congratulatory message like "You're AI Principle #2! Avoid creating or reinforcing unfair bias." At press time, over 34,000 Googlers have played the game.

When it became clear that this lighthearted approach was working, it became a campaign that the team named the Responsible Innovation (RESIN) Challenge. The EngEDU Responsible AI team developed a word search game, a crossword puzzle, and a "guess the emoji" game, all with the goal of socializing the AI Principles. The RESIN Challenge continued gaining momentum and even became part of new-hire orientation. The team also received a larger budget, so it designed a more significant, custom-programmed computer game. Each player travels through a series of scenarios and identifies or applies the appropriate AI principle to win virtual prizes. Over 3,200 Googlers have played it so far, and a second version is in the works. Ultimately, the RESIN Challenge gained the support and endorsement of the most senior Googlers in responsible AI (*https://oreil.ly/FXKOb*).

The EngEDU Responsible AI team began as a single individual who had no budget but a lot of passion for the topic. (Learn more about her story on Google's blog, *The Keyword* (*https://oreil.ly/qSPSp*).) At the start, very few Googlers could name a single AI Principle, but over time, tens of thousands learned to recognize and recall some or all of them. Bottom-up efforts like these are hard work, and they can be successful, even if they don't have a big budget.

Let's review the factors that make the RESIN Challenge a great example of responsible software engineering:

*A responsible goal*
> The team believed that if Google software engineers learned and understood the AI Principles, they would be more likely to implement AI software responsibly.

*Proactivity*
> Nowadays, the RESIN Challenge is shared with new hires at Google so they can learn the AI Principles before they begin any projects.

# Summary

I'm not saying cultural change is easy. It doesn't happen overnight. It takes hard work, legwork, and a commitment to do the right thing for your users. I hope the tips in this chapter help you build and nurture a culture of responsible software engineering in your company.

More broadly, thank you for reading this book. When I speak with individual software engineers about ensuring privacy and safety, optimizing to reduce their code's carbon footprint, and other aspects of responsible software engineering, pretty much everyone I meet understands and supports these efforts. On the whole, people in our profession want to treat our users with respect while we make a living designing systems and writing code. The trick is to actually make it happen when there are so many competing demands and looming deadlines. It takes more time and effort up front to be responsible, but ultimately, it saves us time (in the form of fewer emergencies after launch, easier maintenance, and so on) and it's just the right thing to do for our users and the world. I hope you'll apply the lessons in this book and share them with your teammates and your leaders.

# Index

## A

abstraction, societal context and, 51-52
abuser testing, implementing, 86-88
accessibility, agents with expertise in, 58
accuracy
    fairness vs., 20-21
    issues with, 27, 33-34
ACM (Association for Computing Machinery), 6
action plans, 98
adjustment stage, in Google's review process for responsible AI, 162
agents
    as a component of societal context, 49
    identifying, 57-60
AI Fairness Checklist (Microsoft), 45
AI input, ambiguity of, 24-26
AI output, evaluating, 26
AI Portrait Light (feature), 163
AI principles (AIP) team, 162
AI Principles (Google), 7, 168-171
AI systems, 6, 13-45
"AI Risk Management Framework" (NIST), 7
"AI Smart Practices", 157
Algorithmic Bias Playbook, 57
All Our Wrong Todays (Mastai), 72
Allen Institute for AI, 35
allocative harms, 84
AlphaFold, 86
AlphaGo, 149
Alt tag, 41
Amazon Web Services, 145
Amazon's Building AI Responsibly, 7
ambiguity, of AI input, 24-26, 42

American English, as dominant language in tech, 16
analysis stage, in Google's review process for responsible AI, 161
anonymization
    best practices, 120-122
    definition, 117
    differential privacy (DP), 120-122
    difficulty of, 117
    generalization, 118
    k-anonymity, 119
    obfuscation, 118
    user privacy and, 117-122
Anthropocene (Google), 147
app.electricitymaps.com, 144
Apple
    Exposure Notification System (GAEN), 124-128
    Maps, 126
applications
    profiling, 142
    stress-testing, 88
area under the receiver operating characteristic curve (AUC-ROC), 66
Ariane 5 rocket, 6, 74
artifacts
    as a component of societal context, 49
    identifying, 57-60
Association for Computing Machinery (ACM), 6
assumptions, bias in basic, 23
asterisk (*) argument, 24
AUC-ROC (area under the receiver operating characteristic curve), 66

auto-evaluation, 26
awareness of responsible engineering principles, measuring, 167

## B

benchmarking, 56
best practices
    anonymization (differential privacy), 120-122
    anticipating consequences, 82-90
    carbon footprint of code, 140-148
    fairness, 36-40
    for internal sites, 158
    societal context, 57-64
bias
    during operation of AI systems, 23
    fairness issues and, 14
    in basic assumptions, 23
    in selecting training data, 23
    in training data, 23
    mitigating in care management algorithm, 56-57
    presence of, 22-23
bias amplification, 42
"Bias and Fairness in Large Language Models: A Survey", 45
Big Tech, 124, 136, 147
the blind spot, 23
The Blind Spot: Why Science Cannot Ignore Human Experience (Frank, Gleiser, and Thompson), 23
"Blueprint for an AI Bill of Rights", 7
Bluetooth devices, 126
BPTK-Py, 56
breadth
    in stakeholders, 59
    testing with, 82-83
British Post Office, 74
Building AI Responsibly (Amazon), 7
Buolamwini, Joy, 15
Burgess, Anthony, 129

## C

calculator, greenhouse gas equivalencies, 136
capacity management, 143
carbon dioxide equivalent (CO2e), 135
carbon emissions, measuring, 132-140
carbon footprint, 131-150
    controlling, 140-147

measuring carbon emissions, 132-140
    measuring changes in, 168
    principles of power, 134-138
    scopes one, two, and three, 139
Carbon Footprint tool (Google), 144
carbon intensity metric, 145
carbon neutral, 145
carbon-free energy percentage (%CFE), 145
Carbon-Intelligent Computing System (Google), 146
care management algorithm, mitigating bias in, 56-57
cartoon characters, 4
case studies
    colorized photos, 33
    cooling data centers with AI, 148-150
    detecting toxic comments, 64-69
    Google's Moral Imagination Workshop, 90-99
    health care algorithm, 47-48, 56-57
    launching AI Portrait Light, 163
    making AlphaFold open source, 86
    oversexualized generated imagery, 41-45
    preventing gender bias in Google Ads, 30
    profiling applications, 142
    protecting privacy during the COVID pandemic, 124-128
    Responsible Innovation Challenge, 168-171
    sharing the impact on customers, 154
    Six Thinking Hats, 64
    where did Jesus go?, 77
Casual Conversations dataset, 35
causal assumption
    defined, 52
    explicitness of, 52-56
causal loop diagram, 55
%CFE (carbon-free energy percentage), 145
chaos engineering, 89
"Click to Cancel" rule, 156
CO2e (carbon dioxide equivalent), 135
coaching, agents with expertise in, 59
code
    controlling location in data centers, 144-146
    for performance, 143
code profiler, 141
codelab, 122
codesigning, with users, 83
collaboration (see cross-cultural collaboration)
collaborators, 55

Collingridge dilemma, 73
complexity, in adopting a responsible mindset, 9
consent
    GAEN and, 128
    user privacy and, 111-113
consequences, methods for anticipating, 82-90
context, fairness and, 22
control, user privacy and, 113-115
cookies, dark pattern, 112
counterfactual fairness, 27-28
    Google Search and, 77
    Perspective API and, 66
crash cart, 71
Creative Commons, 161
cross-functional collaboration
    of GAEN, 127
    Perspective API and, 69
    responsible software engineering and, 150
CrowdStrike outage, 6
culture of responsibility, 154-157
culture-building, 151-171
    creating incentives, 163-166
    establishing processes, 161-163
    learning from mistakes, 166
    measuring success, 167-168
    setting policy, 152-157
    spreading the word, 157-161
curb-cut effect, 15
curiosity, in adopting a responsible mindset, 9
Cwip, the clever, well-intentioned person (character), 4

## D

dark pattern, 112
data collection, 105-107
data minimization, 115-116
data perspective
    data collection from the, 107
    user privacy from, 115-122
data retention, 116-117
dataset, 35, 66-69, 117-122
de Bono, Edward, 62
decentralized data collection, GAEN and, 128
decision stage, in Google's review process for responsible AI, 162
deep reinforcement learning, 148
demographic parity, as a fairness metric, 17
Design for Safety (PenzeyMoog), 86

Detecting Toxic Comments case study, 64-69
"Developing a Framework for Responsible Innovation", 159
differential privacy (DP), 120-122
Digital Markets Act (DMA), 7
Disaster Recovery Testing (DiRT), 89
DMA (Digital Markets Act), 7
Doctorow, Cory, 103
domain experts, GAEN and, 127
downstream consequences, 71-99
    methods for anticipating consequences, 82-90
    safety and harm, 73-82
DP (differential privacy), 120-122
DuckDuckGo, 128

## E

EARR (Equitable AI Research Roundtable) (Google), 37
education, 89
    consistent vocabulary, 157
    ethics and safety, 159
    of new hires, 159-161
    publishing articles (AI Smart Practices), 157
embeddings, 30
Endy, the end user (character), 5
EngEDU (Engineering Education, Google), 169-171
Environmental Insights Explorer (Google), 132, 147
Environmental Protection Agency (EPA), 136
environments
    creating for exchanging viewpoints, 60-62
    trusting and supportive, 60
EPA (Environmental Protection Agency), 136
equal opportunity, in adopting a responsible mindset, 9
equality of opportunity, as a fairness metric, 17
equality of service, as a fairness metric, 17
Equitable AI Research Roundtable (EARR) (Google), 37
ethics
    relationship with safety, 78-79
    sidestepping, 80-82
Ethics in Tech Practice: A Toolkit, 161
European Union (EU), 7
    Artificial Intelligence Act, 7
    General Data Protection Regulation (GDPR), 103

executive order, on safe AI, 7
experience, of team members, 37
experts, scaled evaluations and, 40
Exposure Notification System (GAEN), 124-128
Exposure Notifications, 124-128
external sentiment about a company, measuring, 168

# F

FaaS (function as a service), 135
FACET image dataset, 35
facial recognition system, 15
facilitator, having a strong, 61
failure library, 167, 168
Fair-speech dataset, 35
"Fairness and Abstraction in Sociotechnical Systems", 45
fairness issues, 14-18
  accuracy vs., 20-21
  best practices, 36-40
  beyond race and gender, 16
  difficulty of, 18-26
  evaluating, 26-36
  mitigating, 36-40
  relative nature of, 21-22
  resources for evaluating, 35
false positives, 17
Fitzpatrick scale, 35
444 argument, chmod command, 24
frame problem, 26
Frank, Adam, The Blind Spot: Why Science Cannot Ignore Human Experience, 23
function as a service (FaaS), 135
Fundamental Law of Information Recovery, 122
future regret, 85

# G

GAEN (Exposure Notification System), 124-128
GCP (Google Cloud Platform), 144
GDPR (General Data Protection Regulation), 7, 103
gender bias, learned, 30
gender, fairness and, 16
General Data Protection Regulation (GDPR), 7, 103

generalization, as an anonymization technique, 118-119
generative AI systems, 6, 26, 72, 158
GitHub repository on DP, 122
Gleiser, Marcelo, The Blind Spot: Why Science Cannot Ignore Human Experience, 23
Google
  AI Principles, 7, 168-171
  Anthropocene, 147
  blog, 170
  Carbon Footprint tool, 144
  Carbon-Intelligent Computing System, 146
  case studies, 8
  climate change projects at, 132
  colorized photos, 33
  curb-cut effect at, 16
  Disaster Recovery Testing (DiRT), 89
  Engineering Education (EngEDU) team, 157, 171
  Environmental Insights Explorer, 132, 147
  Equitable AI Research Roundtable (EARR), 37
  Exposure Notification System (GAEN), 124-128
  Jigsaw, 64, 167
  Machine Learning Crash Course, 36
  machine learning fairness training, 36
  Model Card Toolkit, 39
  Monk Skin Tone Dataset, 35
  Moral Imagination Workshop, 90-99
  oversexualized generated imagery case study, 41-45
  Principles Pioneers at, 37
  Privacy Policy, 111
  Project Sunroof, 132, 147
  Responsible AI team, 168-171
  review process for responsible AI, 161
  Societal Context Understanding Tools and Solutions (SCOUTS), 67
  TIDAL database, 69
Google Ads, 30
Google Assistant, 40, 76, 77, 83
Google Cloud, 144, 154
Google Cloud Platform (GCP), 144
Google DeepMind, 86, 148, 154, 159
Google Images, 114
Google Maps, 51, 126, 147
Google Photos app, 163
Google Street View, 116

176 | Index

Google Voice, 1, 74
Googler, 141, 147, 157-158, 166, 170
governance, 152
graphics processing unit (GPU), 140, 143
Green Software Foundation, 147
Greenhouse Gas Equivalencies Calculator, 136

# H
harm
    exercises to predict, 98
    types of (taxonomy), 74, 84
harm amplification, 42
harmful associations, 30-32
health care, 47-49, 52-57, 71, 80, 104
Health Insurance Portability and Accountability Act (HIPAA), 104
hidden files, 24
HIPAA (Health Insurance Portability and Accountability Act), 104
How to Be Perfect: The Correct Answer to Every Moral Question (Schur), 79
humility
    in adopting a responsible mindset, 9
    Perspective API and, 69

# I
identity protection, GAEN and, 128
IEA (International Energy Agency), 132
IEEE (Institute of Electrical and Electronics Engineers), 7
IMDB (Internet Movie Database), 119
implicit associations, 30-32
impossibility theorem, 18
Imprisoned in English: The Hazards of English as a Default Language (Wierzbicka), 16
incentives, creating, 163-166
incidents, counting, 168
Inclusion Champions, 37
input (AI), ambiguity of, 24-26
Institute of Electrical and Electronics Engineers (IEEE), 7
intake stage, in Google's review process for responsible AI, 161
internal search engine, testing with, 158
International Energy Agency (IEA), 132
Internet Explorer (Microsoft), 85
Internet Movie Database (IMDB), 119
interpersonal harms, 84
IP addresses, 105

# J
Jesus, missing search results incident, 76
Jigsaw (Google), 64-69, 167
    (see also Perspective API)

# K
k-anonymity, 119
The Keyword (blog), 170
kilowatt hours (kWh), 134
kilowatts (kW), 134
knowledge
    measuring, 167
    of team members, 37
kW (kilowatts), 134
kWh (kilowatt hours), 134

# L
language
    agents with expertise in, 58
    fairness and, 16
law, agents with expertise in, 58
legal privacy, 102
lenses, 159
list of values, 91
LOOPY, 56

# M
machine learning (ML), 15, 36, 158
Machine Learning Crash Course (Google), 36
maintenance plans, 158
marked language, 14, 38-39
Martin, Donald, Jr., 67
Mastai, Elan, All Our Wrong Todays, 72
Meadows, Donella H., Thinking in Systems: A Primer, 56
measurements, suggested for evaluating fairness, 26
megawatt hour (MWh), 138
megawatts (MW), 138
messaging, 157-158
Meta
    AI datasets from, 35
    Responsible AI, 7
Microsoft
    AI Fairness Checklist, 45
    Internet Explorer, 85
    Responsible AI Standard, 7
Microsoft Azure, 145

Index | 177

Microsoft Tay, 83
minimization
    GAEN and, 128
    user privacy and, 115-116
mistakes, learning from, 166
mitigating
    bias in care management algorithm, 56-57
    fairness issues, 36-40
ML (machine learning), 15, 36, 158
MLCommons, 35
Model Card Toolkit (Google), 39
model cards, 39
model collapse, 42
modified dataset, 121
Monk Skin Tone Dataset, 35
moral imagination workshop, 90-99
mutual distrust model, 149
MW (megawatts), 138
MWh (megawatt hour), 138

## N

National Institute of Standards and Technology
    (NIST), 7
natural language, 25
NCEI (nonconsensual explicit imagery), 114
Netflix Challenge contest, 119
The New York Times, 65
NIST (National Institute of Standards and
    Technology), 7
no one right answer (NORA), 21, 25, 29
nonconsensual explicit imagery (NCEI), 114
Noogler, 159
NORA (no one right answer), 21, 25, 29

## O

obfuscation, 118-119
100% renewable energy, 146
operating system (OS), 5
operation of AI systems, bias during, 23
opportunity, equality of, 17
optimizing code execution, for time of day, 146
organizational culture, 77
original dataset, 121
OS (operating system), 5
output (AI), evaluating, 26
oversexualized generated imagery case study,
    41-45

## P

parity issues, 26, 27-30, 33-34
PenzeyMoog, Eva, Design for Safety, 86
people-related suggestions, for mitigating fair-
    ness issues, 36-38
performance, coding for, 143
Perfy Award, 141
personally identifiable information (PII), 104
Perspective API, 66, 68, 73, 167
    (see also Jigsaw (Google))
PII (personally identifiable information), 104
Pixel Camera app, 163
Pixel phone, 163
playful behavior, in videos, 23
policy
    experts in, 58
    scaled evaluations and, 40
    setting, 152-157
portability trap, 39
Post Office Horizon scandal, 74
postmortem, 166
power
    calculating average, 136
    principles of, 134-138
power usage effectiveness (PUE), 145, 148
precepts
    as a component of societal context, 49
    identifying, 57-60
Principles Pioneers (Google), 37
privacy (see user privacy)
Privacy Policy (Google), 111
proactivity
    in adopting a responsible mindset, 8
    in avoiding bias, 30
    Perspective API and, 68
    RESIN Challenge and, 171
process cards, 159
process-related suggestions, for mitigating fair-
    ness issues, 36-38
processes, establishing responsible, 161-163
processor usage, controlling, 140-143
product teams, measuring engagement by, 168
profiling applications, 142
Project Sunroof (Google), 132, 147
proxy service, 105
psychology, experts in, 59
PUE (power usage effectiveness), 145, 148
PySD, 56

178 | Index

# Q

quality assurance (QA), 36
quality, describing responsibility as, 153, 164, 165
quality-of-service harms, 84

# R

race condition, 6
race, fairness and, 16
radiation (see Therac-25 radiation therapy machine)
real-time interaction, in tabletop exercises, 86
recursive operation, chmod command, 24
red teaming, 39-40
Ree, the software engineer (character), 4
reinforcement learning (RL), 43, 148
relativity, of fairness, 21-22
representation harms, 84
RESIN (Responsible Innovation) Challenge, 170
Responsibility and Safety Council (Google DeepMind), 154
responsibility, culture of, 154-157
Responsible AI (Meta), 7
Responsible AI Standard (Microsoft), 7
responsible goals
    Perspective API and, 68
    RESIN Challenge and, 171
    responsible software engineering and, 150
Responsible Innovation (RESIN) Challenge, 170
responsible mindset, adopting a, 8-10
responsible software engineering, 1-4
    definition, 2
    good engineering versus, 5-6
    history of, 6-8
retention, user privacy and, 116-117
revenge porn, 114
risk score, 47
RL (reinforcement learning), 43, 148
robust applications, 36
rocket explosion (see Ariane 5 rocket)
role-playing sessions, 97
-R option (recursive operation, chmod command), 24
Rosenstein, Justin, vii

# S

safety
    describing responsibility as, 153, 164, 165
    relationship to ethics, 78-79
    responsible software engineering and, 150
    testing for, 75-76
scaled evaluations, performing, 40
scenarios for moral imagination, creating, 97
Schneier, Bruce, 103
Schur, Michael, How to Be Perfect: The Correct Answer to Every Moral Question, 79
SCOUTS (Societal Context Understanding Tools and Solutions), 67
SCR (Societal Context Repository), 67
security, GAEN and, 128
serious behavior, in videos, 23
service, equality of, 17
"Simple Demographics Often Identify People Uniquely" study, 118
Six Thinking Hats, 62, 64
Sloss, Ben Treynor, 154
The Social Dilemma, vii
social privacy, 103
social system harms, 84
societal context, 49-51
    best practices, 57-64
    incorporating, 47-69
    issues of abstraction, 51-52
    mitigating bias in care management algorithm, 56-57
Societal Context Repository (SCR), 67
Societal Context Understanding Tools and Solutions (SCOUTS), 67
"Sociotechnical Harms of Algorithmic Systems: Scoping a Taxonomy for Harm Reduction", 84, 98
"The Software Engineering Code of Ethics and Professional Practice", 7
sponsorship, culture of responsibility, 153
stationary Bluetooth beacon, 126
statistical technique, measuring bias, 66
Stella Architect, 56
stereotyping issues, 27, 30-32, 33-34
stress-testing applications, 88
structured data, scaled evaluations and, 40
subgroup accuracy, 21
support, for culture of responsibility, 153
surprises, user privacy and, 108-110
survivor testing, implementing, 86-88

Index | 179

Sweeney, Latanya, 118
system dynamics, 53, 55

## T

tabletop exercises, 85
TDP (thermal design power), 136
technological privacy, 102
technology solutions, for mitigating fairness
    issues, 38-40
Tensor Processing Units (TPU), 140
test sets and metrics, 67
testing
    abuser and survivor, 86-88
    with breadth, 82-83
    with generative AI, 158
    with internal search engine, 158
Therac-25 radiation therapy machine, 6, 74
thermal design power (TDP), 136
Thinking in Systems: A Primer (Meadows), 56
Thompson, Evan, The Blind Spot: Why Science
    Cannot Ignore Human Experience, 23
TIDAL (Google), 69
"TIDE: Textual Identity Detection for Evaluat-
    ing and Augmenting Classification and Lan-
    guage Models", 69
time of day, optimizing for, 146
tool cards, 159
TPU (Tensor Processing Units), 140
trade-offs, 105-107
training data
    bias in, 23
    bias in selecting, 23
    Perspective API and, 69
transparency, user privacy and, 110
trust, user privacy and, 107
trusting and supportive environment, 60
24/7 carbon-free, 146

## U

ungrounded inferences, as a parity issue, 29-30
"Unintended Bias and Identity Terms", 67

updating, simplicity of, 158
US Census Bureau, 121
US Department of Commerce, 7
US Department of Defense, 7
US Federal Trade Commission, 156
user experience (UX)
    experts in, 58
    research, 89
    studies, 83
user perspectives
    data collection from the, 106
    user privacy from, 107-115
    variety of, 61
user privacy, 101-129
    data collection, trade-offs, and convenience,
        105-107
    experts in, 58
    from data perspective, 115-122
    from user's perspective, 107-115
    personally identifiable information (PII),
        104
    tools and policy and, 123
user trust, GAEN and, 127
users, codesigning with, 83

## V

Verily (Alphabet company), 83
Verily Retinal Camera, 83
viewpoints, creating environments for exchang-
    ing, 60-62
volunteering, 89

## W

W (watts), 134
Waymo (Alphabet company), 88
Weld, William, 118
Wierzbicka, Anna, Imprisoned in English: The
    Hazards of English as a Default Language,
    16
Wikipedia, 65
Wing (Alphabet company), 88

## About the Author

**Daniel J. Barrett**, PhD, has been a software engineer and technical writer for almost 40 years at companies of all sizes, from start-ups to large corporations, including 7 years at Google. In addition to *Responsible Software Engineering*, Dan has written numerous other O'Reilly books such as *Linux Pocket Guide*, *Efficient Linux at the Command Line*, *Macintosh Terminal Pocket Guide*, *MediaWiki*, *Linux Security Cookbook*, and *SSH, the Secure Shell: The Definitive Guide*. Learn more by visiting *DanielJBarrett.com*.

## Colophon

The animal on the cover of *Responsible Software Engineering* is the meerkat (*Suricata suricatta*), one of the smallest species in the *Herpestidae* family of mongooses.

Native to the open plains and savannas of southern Africa, meerkats live in tight-knit packs of 2 to 30 individuals—called *mobs* or *gangs*—that cooperate for survival. Each mob may be made up of several families, with each family typically consisting of a breeding pair and their offspring.

Meerkats take a notable amount of responsibility toward educating their young. According to Alex Thornton and Katherine McAuliffe in the journal *Science* (*https://oreil.ly/U5llJ*), adult meerkats explicitly teach their young how to kill or disable prey by giving them injured animals to practice on. The adults even monitor their young's progress.

Meerkats are a fairly ancient species, having been around since not too long after the time of the last dinosaurs. In fact, meerkat fossils dating back as far as 0.01 to 2.59 million years have been discovered. In all that time, the species has had ample opportunity to develop several unique adaptations to their arid environment, including large, curved foreclaws for burrowing; a specialized internal thermoregulation system; and complex social behaviors.

With a relatively widespread geographic range and stable population, the meerkat has been designated by the International Union for Conservation of Nature as being of least concern, from a conservation standpoint. Many of the animals on O'Reilly covers are endangered; all of them are important to the world.

The cover illustration is by Karen Montgomery, based on an antique line engraving from Lydekker's *Royal Natural History*. The series design is by Edie Freedman, Ellie Volckhausen, and Karen Montgomery. The cover fonts are Gilroy Semibold and Guardian Sans. The text font is Adobe Minion Pro; the heading font is Adobe Myriad Condensed; and the code font is Dalton Maag's Ubuntu Mono.

# O'REILLY®

# Learn from experts. Become one yourself.

60,000+ titles | Live events with experts | Role-based courses
Interactive learning | Certification preparation

Try the O'Reilly learning platform free for 10 days.

www.ingramcontent.com/pod-product-compliance
Lightning Source LLC
Jackson TN
JSHW052057070925
90590JS00005B/6